CREATION SPIRITUALITY

Also by Matthew Fox

The Coming of the Cosmic Christ:
The Healing of Mother Earth and the
Birth of a Global Renaissance

Original Blessing: A Primer in Creation Spirituality

Illuminations of Hildegard of Bingen

Hildegard of Bingen's Book of Divine Works,
with Letters and Songs (editor)

Meditations with Meister Eckhart

Breakthrough: Meister Eckhart's
Creation Spirituality in New Translation

A Spirituality Named Compassion
(and the Healing of the Global Village,
Humpty Dumpty and Us)

Western Spirituality:
Historical Roots, Ecumenical Routes (editor)

Whee! We, wee All the Way Home:
A Guide to Sensual, Prophetic Spirituality

On Becoming a Musical, Mystical Bear:
Spirituality American Style

Manifesto for a Global Civilization (with Brian Swimme)

Religion USA: An Inquiry into
Religion and Culture by Way of Time *Magazine*

CREATION SPIRITUALITY

LIBERATING GIFTS FOR THE PEOPLES OF THE EARTH

MATTHEW FOX

HarperSanFrancisco

A Division of HarperCollins*Publishers*

Library of Congress Cataloging-in-Publication Data

Fox, Matthew, 1940–
    Creation spirituality: liberating gifts for the peoples of the
earth / Matthew Fox.—1st ed.
          p.   cm.
    Includes bibliographical references.
    ISBN 0-06-062916-9 (alk. paper).—ISBN 0-06-062917-7 (pbk. : alk.
paper)
    1. Spirituality—Catholic Church.   2. Spiritual life—Catholic
authors.   3. Creation.   4. Liberation theology.   5. Catholic Church—
Doctrines.   I. Title.
BX2350.65.F69   1990
248.4′82 — dc20   90-55298
                                                                                    CIP

94   95   HAD   10   9   8   7   6   5

This edition is printed on acid-free paper that meets the American
National Standards Institute Z39.48 Standard.

To my sisters and brothers in Central and South America who struggle courageously for justice and human rights in society and church: that we may be as keen on learning their courage as they are on learning cosmology from us. And that together we may forge a spirituality of the Americas.

To my mother, Beatrice Sill Fox, in gratitude for her gifts of wisdom so evident in her passion for wonder and for liberation.

To Michael Murray (1947–1990) of Indianapolis, Indiana, and Flint, Michigan, who struggled all his life for the liberation of many—including himself—and who gifted us with a unique expression of mystic and prophet.

Contents

Preface

For some time now people have been asking me for an essay that would both outline the basics of creation spirituality for beginners and challenge seasoned practitioners. During my recent sabbatical, I put some effort into such an essay, and the result is this short book.

While on sabbatical I traveled to Holland, Nicaragua, Brazil, Ecuador, New Zealand, and Australia, and if I was awakened to anything during those trips, it is this: The issues that creation spirituality addresses have worldwide significance. I learned, with excitement, that Nicaraguan poet Ernesto Cardenal had just completed an epic poem entitled *Cosmico Cantico* and that Brazilian theologian Leonardo Boff was learning English in order to study today's cosmology. Furthermore, it was exciting to learn that the base community movement in Holland had chosen cosmology, liberation, spirituality, and feminism as their top priorities.

Ecological suffering is common to all parts of the globe and all species on it. This is especially obvious in the two-thirds of the world that is poor. To see the smoke rising from the rain forests of Brazil and to hear firsthand stories about the bounty hunting of the native peoples of the Amazon make vivid connections between ecological and human justice issues. Joanna Macy tells me that she learned that what aroused the people of Hungary and East Germany to assert their rights was the ecological devastation of their countries: "We would rather die of bullets than of choking" was their slogan. With that they marched for their political rights and those of their children. In this context especially I see the recovery of the ancient tradition of creation spirituality as a gift for our times. Perhaps

ecology and cosmology can awaken the rich one-third of the
world as well.

The division of this book into "Gifts of Awe" and "Gifts of
Liberation" is the result of a healthy dialectical dance, not a
dualism. In *On Becoming a Musical, Mystical Bear,* I wrote of the
tension between mysticism (awe) and prophecy (the struggle
for justice). Awe—the mystical response to the cosmos—runs
through all Four Paths of creation spirituality. There is awe in
the beauty and miracle of "isness" (the Via Positiva) and in the
depths of darkness (the Via Negativa); in the novelty of
creativity (the Via Creativa) and in the glory of justice obtained
and compassion retrieved (the Via Transformativa). The awe
comes when the new cosmic story elicits an awakening, a reen-
chantment that is basic to any truly liberating moment or
movement. Experiencing our world in a deeper way heralds a
new relationship to it—especially for those cultures that have
preferred exploitation to wonder.

Awe, then, becomes the first path of the spiritual and mystical journey. Like the second path, the Via Negativa, it is experienced through receptivity, through a kind of nonaction. We
essentially receive awe or darkness or suffering. But, as Anne
Wilson Schaef has observed, among the addicted neither joy
nor pain can be felt. To cut through the addictive enslavement
of overdeveloped cultures is to get to the genuine spiritual
impoverishment of these cultures. The recognition of enslavement is a first step in the liberating process; it is followed by
paths of action that include creativity and acts of passion and
compassion, celebration, and justice making.

Awe therefore leads to liberation; nonaction to action. The
second part of this book, "Gifts of Liberation," applies especially to the one-third of the world that is materially affluent,
although its repercussions would be felt by the poorer peoples
of the world as well. Recently an Australian asked the Peruvian
theologian Gustavo Gutierrez, who is generally considered the
"father" of liberation theology, what liberation theology is for
"First World" peoples.

"I don't know," Gutierrez replied. "I've been working on the liberation of my people. You 'First Worlders' must name liberation for yourselves."

This story lies behind my efforts to elucidate a liberation theology for the so-called "First World" peoples. It has been said that the slave master, as well as the slave, is a victim of slavery. If this is true, then what affects the "Third World" also affects the "First World," although differently. And there lies the rub. The slave could escape slavery by hiding, fleeing, or taking the underground railroad. But how does the slave master escape slavery? Is freeing the slaves enough? What about land, income, family, and relationships to others still bound to the slave system? What about the system itself? Is the slavemaster free if all the *other* slavemasters are still bound to the system of slavery?

I am convinced that liberation theology from the "Third World" cannot free "First World" peoples from themselves. Liberation theology doesn't begin where "First Worlders" need to be moved: from their own self-interest. Because the *contexts* of "First" and "Third" world differ so vastly, the inhabitants of the former need to come to terms with the unique ways in which they are oppressed, as well as the ways in which they contribute to the oppression of others. The implications of a truly liberating theology differ in the "Third World" and the "First World." Liberation theology has often been so bent on its immediate and harrowing agenda of survival in "Third World" countries that it has underestimated the moral and strategic value of feminist and ecological issues, and it has sometimes succumbed to what we might call a patriarchal anthropocentrism (literally, "man-" or "human-centeredness"). It is time therefore for a theology that can liberate "First World" peoples. And it ought to come from our own historical and social context.

The ultimate urge for writing this essay has to come—as all my books have—from deep within myself. As Annie Dillard has put it, "Write as if you are dying." That is the only justification that I, or any writer, can ever offer for cutting down trees to publish one's thoughts or presenting one's gifts to the public. Like Eckhart, who declared he would preach his message to the poor box if no one came to church to hear him, I write because I cannot *not* write about liberating myself and my own people. I write out of a necessity to say a few words about the break-downs—and breakthroughs—our culture is undergoing today. I write because the "First World" has to start freeing itself, and I write about a path called creation spirituality that can guide us toward that freedom.

Despite all the crowing that our politicians and journalists indulge in over the failures of the "Second World" and the breakup of the Soviet Union in our time, our empire—that of "First World" capitalism—is also headed for major upheaval. It is much easier to crow over the crumbling house next door than to take a look at one's own.

Need I list the issues of our day that go virtually unattended to in our culture? Destruction of the soil, forests, water, and air; racism; sexism; adultism that places youth in a cycle of depres- sion, violence, and crime; an educational system that doesn't work for the nearly 50 percent of our city youth who drop out of high school; the breakdown of the family; our contribution to "Third World" indebtedness; militarism as the backbone of our economic system; the billion-dollar Savings and Loan rip-off; the Housing and Urban Development scandal; home- lessness; the income gap between rich and poor; religious scandals; fundamentalism; the worldwide increase in the popu- larity of fascist movements; drugs, on which Americans spend $150 billion a year; alcoholism and other addictions; unem- ployment; the list goes on and on.

Amid all this "First World" squalor, the media tell us we are the "land of the free" and our economic system is "the wave of the future." The left wing, on the other hand, urges us to listen to the oppressed and choose a "preferential option for the poor." But what if we have lost our capacity for listening at all? And who are "the poor"? Are women, the young, people of color, drug addicts, workers on minimum wage, artists, forests, soil, water, air, and animals included when we speak of "the poor"? How can we hear the poor? How can we attend to the poverty within ourselves? How do we learn to listen once again?

An *impoverishment of the soul* exists within "First World" countries: the means for a just existence are within our grasp, but our wills, our social structures, and our imaginations have not yet proven adequate for that struggle. I would name the sickness of the "Third World" as an *impoverishment of the body,* in the sense that basic bodily needs—food, housing, health care, and work—are so often lacking. The connection between the soul-sickness of the north and the body-sickness of the south is as strong as the connection, within the human organism, of the soul and the body. We are one in our sickness and disease; we will be one in our healing and liberation. What needs healing is different in each case, however; and the remedy for healing and liberation also differs.

In *Fear of Falling,* a perceptive study of middle-class Americans, Barbara Ehrenreich writes, "We need a revival of conscience and responsibility in the middle class. But from what ground is it likely to spring? What crisis might inspire it? What exhortations would have the power to call it forth?" I believe that creation spirituality can assist us in our own liberation and, once awakened, we would more truly support our "Third World" neighbors as they go about their own task of liberation. And we would wake up anew to the material impoverishment and injustice that we have failed to heed in our own countries for so long.

A word about language seems to be in order as we begin this exploration of "First" and "Third" world liberation movements. I do not like either of these terms, for the simple reason that they betray an obvious bias—why is the two-thirds of the world that is poor called the "Third World"? And why is it that the 15 percent of the world that consumes 50 percent of its resources called "First"? Needless to say, however, this language, which is political, like all language, tells a story about itself and carries the seeds of truth about our relationships. Throughout this book, I will use the terms "First World" and "Third World"

only in quotation marks. I prefer, in fact, the terms "overdeveloped" and "underdeveloped" world. I consider the "First
World" overdeveloped materially, but underdeveloped spiritually; by contrast the "Third World" is less developed from an
industrial point of view, but healthier spiritually in its passion
for mystery and history, for beauty and justice. The priority
that the quest for justice takes in the "Third World" is proof of
a spiritual maturity that the "First World"—mired in its denial,
consumerism, and boredom—cannot yet match.

I hope this book challenges beginners and practioners along
the path of creation spirituality first by acknowledging and
then by analyzing the spiritual poverty of our culture. If it could
contribute to that cause and to the realization of the dream elu-
cidated in chapter 8, then it will have been worthwhile.

Acknowledgments

I am indebted to many people who assisted in the process of writing this book. Among them are those mentioned in the bibliography, but I also wish to thank the following persons: Leonardo and Clodovis Boff and the thousands of members of the CEBS, or Ecclesial Base Communities, who met outside Rio de Janeiro this summer and allowed us North Americans to "sit in." Thomas and Elvira Hallan, who showed us much Brazilian hospitality and arranged so many rich visits with the brave people of Brazil. Some of these brave people, including Cardinal Evaristo Arns, Bishop Tomás Baldvíno, and Bishop Pedro Cásadaliga, who so warmly opened his home to us. Margaret Buttita, for accompanying us to the "Basin of the Amazon." Jerry Stookey and Mary Alice McCabe, who opened doors for us in Nicaragua, and the brave people there—the groups of *campesinos* organizing cooperatives in the countryside, Ernesto Cardenal, Leana Núñez, and many more. A special thanks to Dom Helder Camera for, among other things, teaching that we need to "stir the consciousness of the rich at home and abroad." Marie Augusta Neal, for saying that "a radical conversion of the nonpoor is needed today." Krister Stendahl, who teaches of the "loss for those who have too much" that needs to be undergone. M. C. Richards, for her conversations on the "impoverishment of the 'First World.'" David Gentry–Akin, my companion on the Brazilian and Nicaraguan journey, who did the initial editing of this book. Thomas Grady, at HarperSanFrancisco. The faculty and staff at the Institute in Culture and Creation Spirituality, who kept the fires burning during my sabbatical year—especially Jim Conlon, Marlene Denardo, and Bob Frager. Brian Swimme and Thomas Berry, for educating me in the new cosmic story. And to that mysterious spirit that made my sabbatical year possible and that never ceases to teach and to surprise.

Prologue:
A New Creation Story

Poet and potter M. C. Richards has commented on what happens when science and religion, which went their separate ways three centuries ago, split apart. "There is palpable disunion," she writes. "This split obstructs the poetic consciousness; it is a characteristic malady of our society. . . . The inner soul withdraws, goes underground, splits off from the part that keeps walking around. Vitality ebbs. Psychic disturbance is acute. Suicide may be attempted."

If this naming of the cultural malady rings true, then imagine what might happen when science and spirituality come together again. That possibility, in fact, constitutes the best and most empowering news of our time. Science today has given us a new cosmic story about our origins. It is a sacred story, one that fills us with awe on hearing it. I will attempt here to tell the story in my fashion. It is a story of gifts; we come from a lineage of cosmic gift giving.

In the beginning was the gift.
And the gift was with God and the gift was God.
And the gift came and set its tent among us,
first in the form of a fireball
that burned unabated for 750,000 years
and cooked in its immensely hot oven
hadrons and leptons.
These gifts found a modicum of stability,
enough to give birth to the first atomic creatures,
hydrogen and helium.
A billion years of stewing and stirring
and the gifts of hydrogen and helium

1

birthed galaxies—spinning, whirling, alive galaxies
created trillions of stars,
lights in the heavens and cosmic furnaces
that made more gifts
through violent explosions of vast supernovas
burning abright with the glow
of more than a billion stars.
Gifts upon gifts, gifts birthing gifts, gifts exploding,
gifts imploding, gifts of light, gifts of darkness.
Cosmic gifts and subatomic gifts.
All drifting and swirling, being born and dying,
in some vast secret of a plan.
Which was also a gift.
One of these supernova gifts exploded in a special manner
sending a unique gift to the universe,
which later-coming creatures would one day call
earth,
their home.
Its biosphere was also a gift,
wrapping it with beauty and dignity and just the right
protection from sun's radiation
and from the cosmic cold.
And eternal night.
This gifted planet was set as a jewel
in its most exquisite setting,
in this case, the exact distance of 100 million miles
from its mother star, the sun.
New gifts arose, never seen in such forms in the universe—
rocks, oceans, continents,
multicellular creatures that moved by their own inner power.
Life was born!
Gifts that had taken the form of fireball and helium,
galaxies and stars, rock and water, now took the form of Life!
Life—a new gift of the universe, a new gift in the universe.
Flowers of multiple color and scent, trees standing upright.
Forests arose offering places for all manner
of creeping, crawling things.

Of things that fly and sing.
Of things that swim and slither.
Of things that run on four legs.
And, eventually,
of things that stand and walk on two.
With thumbs that move to make still more creativity—
more gift making—
possible.
The human became a gift, but also a menace.
For its powers of creativity were unique in their potential
for destruction or healing.
How would humans use these gifts?
Which direction would they choose?
The earth waited for an answer to these questions.
And is still waiting.
Trembling.
Teachers were sent, divine incarnations
birthed from the soil.
Isis and Hesiod, Buddha and Lao Tzu, Moses and Isaiah,
Sara and Esther, Jesus* and Paul,
Mary and Hildegard, Chief Seattle and Buffalo Woman.
To teach the humans ways of compassion.
And still the earth waited
to see if humanity was gift or curse.
Trembling.
Have you ever given a gift and then regretted it afterward?
Earth wonders and waits.
For the gift has been made flesh
and dwells everywhere among us
and we tend to know it not.
And to treat it not as a gift
but as an object.
To be used, abused, trampled underfoot—even crucified.

---

*This attempt to place Jesus in the context of world religions does not
diminish his unique role in Christianity, which is discussed in chapter 4.

But to those who do receive it as a gift
all is promised.
All shall be called children of the gift,
sons and daughters of grace.
For all generations.

PART ONE

GIFTS OF AWE

❖ 1 ❖

What Is Creation Spirituality?

This past year a reporter for the *New York Times* interviewed me in a hotel room in New York City. An African-American woman, she began with: "Look, I grew up in the inner city of Chicago and now I live in Manhattan. What does creation spirituality have to say to me? Is it just about visiting parks and zoos?"

I invited her to look out the window and tell me what she could see. We were on the eighteenth floor and bricks framed the window. What is a brick? Clay raised up eighteen floors by humans. And what keeps the bricks up? Steel girders—also gifts from the earth. We went to the window together and looked down. Below us were numerous taxicabs, all made of steel (also from the bowels of the earth), running on tires made from rubber trees and fuel made from the dead plants and animals from hundreds of millions of years ago. A city—as awesome a place as it is—is also earth, earth recycled by humans who themselves are earth standing on two legs with movable thumbs and immense imaginations.

Creation spirituality is as much a city experience as a rural one provided we are willing to look for the source of things and the relationships among them. In this chapter I will elucidate more fully the path of creation spirituality.

What Is Creation?

Creation is all things and us. It is us in relationship with all things. "All our relations," the Lakota people pray whenever they smoke the sacred pipe or enter or leave the sweatlodge. "All our relations" implies all beings, all things, the ones we see and the ones we do not; the whirling galaxies and the wild suns, the black holes and the microorganisms, the trees and the stars, the fish and the whales, the wolves and the porpoises, the flowers and the rocks, the molten lava and the towering snow-capped mountains, the children we give birth to and their children, and theirs, and theirs, and theirs. The unemployed single mother and the university student, the campesino and the landowner, the frog in the pond and the snake in the grass, the colors of a bright sunny day and the utter darkness of a rain forest at night, the plumage of sparkling parrots and the beat of an African drum, the kiva of the Hopi and the wonder of Chartres Cathedral, the excitement of New York City and the despair of an overcrowded prison are included as well.

Creation is all space, all time—all things past, present, and future. Among these three ways of conceptualizing time, creation leans the most in the direction of the present, for the most significant of the times is in the Now, the "Eternal Now." By the choices we make now about what we birth, the past presses into the future. Whether the future presents itself as still more beauty or as still more pain depends upon our choices as we respond to our role as co-creators in an ever-unfolding creation. In us the past and present come together to birth a future. As Eckhart puts it:

> God is creating the entire universe fully and
> totally in this present now.
> Everything God created six thousand years ago—
> and even previous to that as God made the world—
> God creates now all at once.
> Everything which God created millions of years ago
> and everything which will be created by God
> after millions of years—
> if the world endures until then—
> God is creating all that in the innermost and
> deepest realms of the soul.

Everything of the past and everything of the present
and everything of the future
God creates in the innermost realms of the soul.

Creation, then, at its core, is about relation. It is the spiraling, dancing, crouching, springing, leaping, surprising act of
relatedness, of communing, of responding, of letting go, of
being. Being is about relation. Eckhart says that "relation is the
essence of everything that exists" and that "isness is God." Thus
all creation is a trace, a footprint, an offspring of the Godhead.
Creation is the passing by of divinity in the form of isness. It
is God's shadow in our midst. It is sacred. All our relationships
are sacred. Native peoples know this. Jesus taught it. ("I am the
vine, you are the branches." "My father and I are one.") Christians and other believers must learn anew the sacredness of creation. Without this, the "first article of faith," we are lost. Our
children will be adrift and without a future. Despair rules and
any talk of the "reign of God" lacks energy and truth.

Creation is, in many respects, what our species makes of it
here on earth. How foolish of divinity to give us such divine
and demonic power. What are we doing with it? Are we pre-
pared spiritually for this awesome task of justice making; of
what science terms "homeostasis"—the quest for balance built
into all things; of relating all things at the level of justice and
not of power-over; of winners vs. losers? Have we truly out-
grown war—war against ourselves, our bodies, our youth, our
soil, our trees, ourselves? Humans are quite capable of sinning
against creation, of missing the mark of our purpose in being
on this planet and in this universe. In this sense, sin is a turning
away from creation and its author, the divine one who dwells
in all things. Sometimes we sin by omission—by not realizing
or admitting sins against the biosphere (rightly called ecocide)
or against earth species (biocide) or against the soil (geocide).
Yet these are truly *mortal* sins, for they will prove to be deadly
for generations yet to come.

Creation is the something new that happens when our first
child is born; it is the resurrection we experience when we

bottom out from pain and despair and experience being alive; it is the peace that passes all understanding when a good person dies well; it is the arousal of community spirit that arrives when fear is faced down by solidarity and when powerful prayer and hope become rooted in us again.

Creation is what the mystic is awakened to and what the prophet fights to sustain. Creation is the subject of the scientist's search and mystical commitment, and it is the source of all worship and the goal of all morality. The mystic seeks a New Creation—where the wolf and the lamb in us lie down together, where strength and gentleness are faced and welcomed in hospitality, where animus and anima, male and female, as well as all paradoxes are reconciled in a living, whirling, laugh-filled dance to the erotic Godhead who painted us all, sang us all, gifted us all, imagined us all, and still laughs at us all.

Creation is the source, the matrix, and the goal of all things—the beginning and the end, the alpha and the omega. Creation is our common parent, when "our" stands for all things. Creation is the mother of all beings and the father of all beings, the birther and the begetter. It is all-holy; it is awe-filled, from the tiniest onion seed to the towering redwood tree. It is all-powerful; it resurrects. If just one person has ever been resurrected from the dead, then we all have, and creation is the inheritor of still more divine surprises. Creation is never finished, never satisfied, never bored, never passive. Creation is always newly born, always making new. It entices us as a lover does to a secret place where it alone will play with us until we lose all sense of past, present, and future, and we become at last and in spite of ourselves fully present to all space and all time. From this secret rendezvous with creation, new beings enter the universe and, like newly birthed galaxies, our mystically conceived children spin their own stories of creation into still more time and more space and bigger and brighter orbiting lights and colors.

How can it be that such a drama can be jeopardized as it is today? Only because our species, with its religions, education, moralities, governments, economics, has lost the sense of creation. When that happens, nothing is holy; nothing seems worth the struggle for justice that is necessary to preserve it. Community dies, and relations no longer exist.

Creation spirituality is not centered in psychology, for it is not about the human isolated from *all* our relations. It is, however, blessing centered, where *blessing* means the gift that all creation is. I was recently on a panel with psychologist M. Scott Peck, who remarked that unconditional love lasts only between parents and child until the child is old enough to talk back. In an anthropocentric context, unconditional love is indeed rare; but in a cosmological context it is an everyday occurrence: the universe loves us every day the sun rises, and the creator loves us through creation.

Creation is original blessing, and all the subsequent blessings—those we give our loved ones and those we struggle to bring about by healing, celebration, and justice making—are prefigured in the original blessing that creation is, a blessing so thoroughly unconditional, so fully graced, that we can go through life hardly noticing it at all. Our religions are capable of building their magnificent temples, housing their vast followers, teaching their elaborate catechisms, and raising their considerable sums of money, but forgetting entirely about the grace of creation. Boredom, depression, and what our ancestors called the sin of "acedia" (or ennui) occur when we get cut off from the sense of grace and blessing.

Yes, creation is so foolishly generous that it has birthed, in its effort to be effusively loving, a species that endangers its own home. In its humility, creation has rendered itself subject to one of its own making, the human species. How holy, how extravagant, how wise, and yet how fragile creation is. How will it respond if humanity despoils its earth-expression?

What Is Spirituality?

The Spirit is life, *ruah*, breath, wind. To be spiritual is to be alive, filled with *ruah*, breathing deeply, in touch with the wind. Spirituality is a life-filled path, a spirit-filled way of living.

Taking a path is different from driving down a highway to work. A path has something personal about it; it implies choice or even mystery. To choose one path is to reject another. A path is a meandering walkway—you do not rush or even drive down a pathway. A path is not goal oriented. A path is *the way itself,* and every moment on it is a holy moment; a sacred seeing goes on there.

All who embark on a spiritual path need to be willing to learn and to let go; to know that none of us has all the answers, and yet that none of us is apart from divinity; to be able to let go of bitterness or prolonged anger. We can drive down a freeway and be full of anger, but we cannot walk down a pathway when filled with anger or bitterness. We must be emptied to be able to walk the pathway of spirituality, and of course the walking itself will accomplish its own surprising emptying.

While there is something deeply personal about the paths we choose to walk down, spirituality is also radically communitarian. The Spirit is not bound to a path just because we are on it. Pathways beckon us out of their beauty, but they beckon *us,* not *me,* not *my private ego* hoarding my private property or following my private way. A path is a way of solidarity, of sharing the beauty with all the others on the way; it is also a sharing of the pain and the struggle with all the others on the way.

What is common to all paths that are spiritual is, of course, the Spirit—breath, life, energy. That is why all true paths are essentially one path—because there is only one Spirit, one breath, one life, one energy in the universe. It belongs to none of us and all of us. We all share it. Spirituality does not make us otherworldly; it renders us more fully alive. The path that spirituality takes is a path *away from the superficial into the depths;* away from the "outer person" into the "inner person"; away from the privatized and individualistic into the deeply communitarian. As Eckhart put it, "The outward person is the old person, the earthly person, the person of this world, who grows old 'from day to day.' That person's end is death. . . . The inward person, on the other hand, is the new person, the heavenly person, in whom God shines." To find this "God who shines" in ourselves is to find the Cosmic Christ and to find a life that binds all things together.

Creation Spirituality: A Tradition and a Movement

Creation spirituality, a path that we choose to take that is distinct from other ways offered us, begins with creation and the cosmos. Only later does it get to the human story, which then attracts us like a jewel set in the larger drama of creation itself. There can be no anthropology without cosmology. The human does not exist apart from the stars. Human history cannot be divorced from planetary history, galactic history, and creation's entire unfolding history. The elements of our bodies, the vast and cosmic feelings of grief and sadness we undergo, of ecstasy and joy—all these are part of the history and the size of the universe. We are of galactic size.

Proof of our galactic size is found not only in the fact that we can know that the universe in which we live is one trillion galaxies big, but also in the fact that we are now aware that the universe had to exist for nineteen billion years and be one trillion galaxies large before our species could arrive in it. How do we know this? Because space and time evolved together. If that time sequence was essential for our arrival, so too must the dimensions of the universe necessarily be what they are.

A Tradition

Creation spirituality is not a newly invented path. For twentieth-century Westerners it is a newly *discovered* path because the onslaught of anthropocentric (human-centered) culture that began with the breakup of cosmology at the end of the Middle Ages has left us lost in a mechanized and nonmystical world. To encounter creation spirituality today is like opening a jungle path that has long been covered with thick-rooted plants and bramble. Creation spirituality is an ancient tradition, the oldest tradition in this land for it is the basic spiritual heritage of Native Americans. It is also the basic spiritual heritage of native peoples everywhere, the Celtic peoples of Ireland, Scotland, Wales, and the Rhineland in Germany and the native peoples of Africa and Asia, of the Polynesian islands and New Zealand, or of the aboriginals of Australia. All these peoples had cosmology as the basis of their worship, prayer, economics, politics, and morality. All of them honored the artist in all persons. All expected the divine to burst out of anyplace at anytime.* To see the world this way is to be creation centered.

But creation spirituality is not only endemic to native spiritualities everywhere; it is also the most ancient tradition in the Bible. The Yahwist author (or J) source in the Hebrew Bible is the oldest tradition in that Bible, and its theology is creation-centered theology. So too is much of the prophetic books and all of the wisdom literature, which beautifully express the cosmological, feminist vision of creation spirituality.† These are the scriptures that Jesus knew so well, and so the tradition of creation spirituality is carried into the Christian Bible or "New Testament" in myriad places ranging from the prologue to John's Gospel (so dependent on the wisdom book of Sirach, chapter 24) to the Book of Revelation; from the parables of Jesus so steeped in creation imagery and experience to the preaching of Jesus about the "kingdom" of God—a phrase that biblical scholar Krister Stendahl says deserves to be translated

---

*For example, James Cowan writes about the spirituality of the aboriginals of Australia by noting that "as long as there is no wish to recognize the divinity in all things, then Aboriginal belief will always be regarded as a suspect philosophy grounded in superstition and strange ritual practices." Yet to recognize the divinity in all things is creation-centered theology; it is the tradition of panentheism and the Cosmic Christ.

†See, for instance, the Book of Proverbs, chapter 8: "From everlasting I was firmly set, from the beginning, before earth came into being. The deep was not, when I was born, there were no springs to gush with water" (Prov. 8:23).

as "creation"; from hymns to the Cosmic Christ, which early Christians sang in the first liturgies of the Christian church and which Paul invokes in his letters, to the birth narratives in the Gospels of Matthew and Luke.

Creation spirituality is also found in the Greek fathers of the church, especially in the role that the Cosmic Christ plays in their theology. (For example, Basil of Caesarea says, "The Word of God pervades the creation," and Gregory of Nazianzus says that Christ "exists in all things that are.") But the high point of church history regarding creation spirituality occurred in the great "renaissance" that began in the twelfth century, with mystic-prophets such as Hildegard of Bingen, Francis of Assisi and Thomas Aquinas. Following on their genius came Mechtild of Magdeburg, Meister Eckhart, Julian of Norwich, and Nicolas of Cusa, who carried on this spiritual movement in practice and in theory from the thirteenth to the fifteen centuries. However, with the condemnation of Eckhart in 1329, the handwriting was on the wall: don't mix mystical and prophetic faith; it may get you into trouble. The split between the mystical and the prophetic, marked by that date, has haunted religion ever since. The reformers of the sixteenth century tried to bring this power back, but with mixed success, since the secular world was also deprived of the paradigm of the Cosmic Christ and succumbed to the anticreation bias of the new science and the despoiled religious view. The greed emanating from the rape of the New World was too much for a weakened creation morality to resist. The church's burning of the Dominican scientist-mystic Giordano Bruno at the stake in 1600 and its condemnation of Galileo in 1616 were indications of religion's hostility to a new cosmology, which was something that religion could not control. Science and religion parted ways. Today, however, science is once again interested in the sacred, and creation spirituality provides a bridge between the two.

In Matthew's Gospel, Jesus speaks of how "every scribe who becomes a disciple of the reign of heaven" brings forth things "both old and new" (Matt. 14:51). So too is creation spirituality both old and new. As something old, it is a tradition, literally something that has been "handed on." Creation spirituality has been handed on by the struggle of our ancestors in the communion of saints. It is a living tradition, not a fixed package of dogmatic verities. As something new, it is that movement that mixes the new creation story and our new cultural crises into the tradition, making it come alive again.

A Movement

Creation spirituality is also a *movement*. Those who come into contact with it often become so ecstatic upon encountering this long-lost tradition, this heritage from their own Western roots, this treasure long-buried, that they want to move with it. They want the spirit that liberates their souls to be put to good use in liberating others. They want to set fire to the dry wood, what Hildegard called the "dryness of care-less-ness" that exists in lives, their communities, their institutions. People who encounter the creation spirituality tradition find "wetness" in their lives, and they want to make wet the dry corners of our institutions, work worlds, professions, personal relationships, and religion. They want creation spirituality to influence others and the social movements of our time (*influens*, "to flow into"). Creation spirituality is a movement when it awakens people and their slumbering moral outrage at the folly of our race and offers a creative outlet for the justified anger and the pent-up frustration of ordinary folks.

As a movement, creation spirituality becomes an amazing gathering place, a kind of watering hole for persons whose passion has been touched by the issues of our day—deep ecologists, ecumenists, artists, native peoples, justice activists, feminists, male liberationists, gay and lesbian peoples, animal liberationists, scientists seeking to reconnect science and wisdom, people of prophetic faith traditions—all these groups find in the creation spirituality movement a common language and a common ground on which to stand.*

The Four Paths of Creation Spirituality

The backbone of the creation spirituality tradition is its naming of the spiritual journey in the Four Paths. It is important to be able to name the journey so that people can share in a common language. By naming the journey we are assured that we shall not get stuck in any one of the paths, which can easily happen since each of the paths is deep and powerful.

The Four Paths of the creation spirituality journey represent a distinct paradigm shift from the way in which the spiritual journey was formerly described in the West. Plotinus (A.D. 205–270) identified only three paths: purgation, illumination, and union. Creation spirituality rejects as inadequate this way of naming the spiritual journey. It is not biblical, because Plotinus, a Neoplatonist philosopher and mystic, did not know the Bible at all. These paths leave out delight and pleasure, creativity and justice; their goal is not compassion but contemplation and the turning away from the earth and all that relates us to it.

The Four Paths of creation spirituality tell us *what matters*. We are told in Path One that awe and delight matter; in Path Two that darkness, suffering, and letting go matter; in Path

---

*If biologist Rupert Sheldrake is correct is his hypothesis that a "morphic field" is created by a kind of cumulative memory from the past, then perhaps the creation spirituality movement, because it awakens ancient memories, is an example of an ongoing "morphic resonance" that is resurfacing in human consciousness today. Psychologist June Singer believes that Sheldrake's theory explains how new archetypes emerge in the human collective unconscious: "At first a change in attitude or behavior is difficult, but as more and more individuals change, it becomes progressively easier for other people to do so, and not just through direct influence." When new archetypes arise, human transformation occurs.

Three that creativity and imagination matter; and in Path Four that justice and celebration, which add up to compassion, matter. When the Four Paths are understood in light of the new cosmic story, then a whole civilization can be born because, while the Four Paths tell us what matters, the new creation story tells us why it matters—because it has taken nineteen billion years to bring all these experiences of delight and suffering, of birth and justice-making to this point in history.

The Four Paths also address the question, Where will God, where will the experience of the divine, be found in our time? Creation spirituality responds: the divine will be found in these places:

In *the Via Positiva*. In the awe, wonder, and mystery of nature and of all beings, each of whom is a "word of God," a "mirror of God that glistens and glitters," as Hildegard of Bingen put it. This is Path One.

In *the Via Negativa*. In darkness and nothingness, in the silence and emptying, in the letting go and letting be, and in the pain and suffering that constitute an equally real part of our spiritual journey. This is Path Two.

In *the Via Creativa*. In our generativity we co-create with God; in our imaginative output, we trust our images enough to birth them and ride them into existence. This is Path Three.

In *the Via Transformativa*. In the relief of suffering, in the combatting of injustice, in the struggle for homeostasis, for balance in society and history, and in the celebration that happens when persons struggling for justice and trying to live in mutuality come together to praise and give thanks for the gift of being and being together. This is Path Four.

The Four Paths as Four Commandments

One way of grasping the Four Paths of creation spirituality is to understand them as Four Commandments that can energize us for the journey. They are signposts, reassurances that we are not traveling alone but with the entire mystical body: the communion of saints and the creation spirituality tradition, past, present, and future. With this body, the entire movement of creation spirituality journeys along a spiral path. Let's consider these commandments briefly here:

1. *Thou Shalt Fall in Love at Least Three Times a Day (Via Positiva)*

At first glance, this commandment sounds troublesome for one's marriage, relationship, or vow of celibacy, but that's because our anthropocentric culture has taken the immensely mystical experience of "falling in love" and applied it exclusively to finding a mate. In fact, we could fall in love with a galaxy every day and, since there are one trillion of them, bequeath many quite virginal on our deathbed. Or we could fall in love with a star, of which there are 200 billion in our galaxy alone. Or a species of wildflower, of which there are at least 10,000 on this planet. Or a species of bird, of fish, of tree, of plant. Or with another human being—preferably one different from ourselves or suffering differently, such as a Salvadoran, if one is North American and prone to make war on El Salvador. Or a homosexual, if one is proud of being heterosexual. Or black, if one is white, and vice versa. We could fall in love with music, poetry, painting, dance. If we fell in love with one of Mozart's works each week, we would have seven years of joy. How could we ever be bored?

Yes, creation has much to do with falling in love. The creation spirituality journey begins with awe, wonder, and falling in love. The first commandment, the Via Positiva, is that of praise that flows from beholding the awe of our being here.

2. *Thou Shalt Dare the Dark (Via Negativa)*

Meister Eckhart says that "the ground of the soul is dark." This implies that there is no moving from superficiality to depth— and every spiritual journey is about moving from the surface to the depths—without entering the dark. Eckhart also says that "God is superessential darkness"—so there is no encountering the divinity merely in the light. The divine is to be met in the depths of darkness as well as in the light. Daring the dark means entering nothingness and letting it be nothingness while it works its mystery on us. Daring the dark also means allowing pain to be pain and learning from it.

In the pathway that is the Via Negativa, we enter the shadow, the hidden or covered-up parts of ourselves and our society. In doing so, we confront the cover-up that often accompanies evil in self or society. "It is part of an unjust society to cover up the pain of its victims," notes theologian Dorothy Solee. This commandment requires that spiritual voyagers not only let go of cover-up and denial, but that they actually enter into the darkness that pain is all about. Since both despair and apathy arise from the cover-up of anger, this journey of letting go is also one of going deeper than the despair, apathy, bitterness, and cynicism that can create such resentment in our souls and society.

The mystics talk of the "dark night of the soul," which we all taste because we are all mystics, and we all undergo deep darkness. Entering the dark constitutes a necessary part of the journey beyond despair and numbing. Joanna Macy writes: "Experience the pain. Let us not fear its impact on ourselves or others. We will not shatter, for we are not objects that can break." As she points out, the darkness is deeply communitarian: "We are in grief together." It is when the heart is broken that compassion can begin to flow through it.

A return to the dark is also a return to our origins; we were all conceived in the dark, lived our first nine months in the dark, and were from all eternity in the dark heart of the Godhead that preceded the creation of fire and light. The dark mystery of the Godhead calls us all to dare the dark.

Part of darkness is the absence of words and images and the presence of silence. Silence beckons us from the dark. "What preceded the Word?" asks the poet and potter M. C. Richards. Silence and the receptivity that listening to silence brings about. The poet Rilke wrote, "Being silent. Who keeps innerly silent, touches the roots of speech." Path Two is about building up our muscles of receptivity and subtraction, our being at home in the dark, our letting go and letting be.

3. Do Not Be Reluctant to Give Birth (Via Creativa)

This commandment is actually from the diary of psychologist Otto Rank, who wrote the entry when he was sixteen. Rank had been sexually abused as a child and had often considered suicide as a teenager. The advice he wrote to himself was his alternative, and the fruits of this philosophy were amazing, for when he became an adult, he dedicated himself to healing and liberating the wounded artists of his day. It was Rank who said "pessimism comes from the repression of creativity."

All Four Paths of creation spirituality find their apex in Path Three, the Via Creativa. Paths One and Two lead up to Path Three (for we create only out of what we have beheld of light and darkness), and Path Four, the Via Transformativa, flows out of the Via Creativa, since we are putting our imaginations and creativity at the service of compassion.

The basic spiritual discipline in the creation tradition is decidedly not asceticism, but the development of the aesthetic. Beauty, and our role in co-creating it, lie at the heart of the spiritual journey. In Path Three we learn what Eckhart meant when he said that "we are heirs of the fearful creative power of God." Creativity is not about painting a picture or producing an object; it is about wrestling with the demons and angels in the depths of our psyches and daring to name them, to put them where they can breathe and have space and we can look at them. This process of listening to our images and birthing them allows us to embrace our "enemies"—that is, the shadow side of ourselves—as well as to embrace our biggest visions and dreams. Art-as-meditation becomes the basic prayer form in the practice of creation spirituality.

Our culture often intimidates us when it comes to becoming the artists we are meant to be. This commandment cuts through that intimidation. Since the masochist in us is the one who says, "I can't do it, I can't create," Path Three breaks through masochism. But because the masochist needs a sadist, one who says, "You can't, but I can," Path Three also confronts sadism. As Ernesto Cardenal, the former cultural minister of

Nicaragua put it, "people do not consume culture; they create it." A culture is an environment where creativity is honored as a great value, where it happens around and through the people.

The *imago dei* or image of God in all persons is necessarily the image of the Creator. To give birth is to enter the Creator's realm, the work of co-creation as we assist nature and history in carrying on the creativity of the universe.

4. *Be You Compassionate As Your Creator in Heaven Is Compassionate* (*Via Transformativa*)

You may recognize this commandment as coming directly from Jesus' Sermon on the Mount in Luke's Gospel (6:36). It represents the summation of his teaching, and it corresponds to that well-worn sentence in Matthew's version of the Sermon on the Mount that is often translated as "Be you perfect as your Creator in heaven is perfect" (5:48). The problem with this translation is that the word *perfect* does not convey the true sense of the word in Jesus' language. A better translation would be ripe or mature or full. In the Jewish consciousness, such ripeness or fullness would consist in being compassionate as the Divine One is compassionate. Thus, to be perfect is to be compassionate.*

The creation spirituality journey culminates in compassion—the combination of justice making and celebration. Justice and joy equally make up the experience that compassion is about. The capacity to experience our interconnectedness concerns both the joy and the sorrow that we undergo with others. In compassion, "peace and justice kiss," as the psalmist puts it (Ps. 85:10). Compassion is about the actions that flow from us as a result of our interdependence.

---

*Another translation for this word, as Neil Douglas-Klotz has shown in *Prayers of the Cosmos,* would be "all-embracing." Our creator God is "all-embracing" and we ought to be the same. Compassion is all-embracing because it is a response to our interdependence with all things.

To be compassionate is also to be prophetic. Path Four is the path in which all are anointed as prophets, and the prophet, as Rabbi Heschel teaches, "interferes." The prophet interferes with the injustice, the unnecessary pain, that rains on the earth and its creatures when humans neglect justice and compassion. That prophetic call to interfere with injustice resides in all of us.

It is important to recall that justice is a cosmic category as well as a human one. All creation is ruled by justice or homeo-stasis, the quest for equilibrium that is intrinsic to all atoms, galaxies, the earth, the whole history of the universe. The human call to compassion and justice making is not a burden and has nothing to do with feelings of righteousness. It is a matter of the human species joining the dance of all creation in the quest for balance.

The Four Paths as a Sacred Hoop

The special relationships that exist between and among the Four Paths can best be seen if we conceive of them as a sacred hoop corresponding to the four directions.

Paths One and Three, the Via Positiva and the Via Creativa, are related in a special way because they are both about awe and wonder, delight and beauty. Path One is the delight and wonder engendered by the experience of creation itself; Path Three can evoke delight and wonder *at what humans birth*. After all, we are creation too. For example, a thunderstorm is awe-some, but so too is Beethoven's naming of it in his Sixth Sym-phony. His music recalls the holy "isness" of a thunderstorm and rekindles feelings and memories we have of thunder-storms. Thus it can be said that through the Via Creativa we actually increase the amount of awe in the universe. Consider the awesomeness of a bridge or of a jet plane that flies through the air at speeds greater than that of a hurricane; or the send-ing of a satellite to Neptune that, after ten years of travel through space, sends photos from Neptune that require four to six hours just to return to earth.

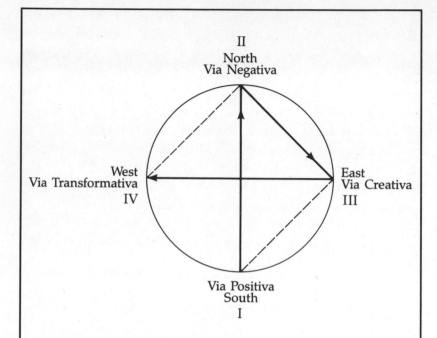

One way of envisioning the Four Paths as a sacred hoop is to see the Via Positiva as South (the direction from which light derives) and the Via Creativa as East (the direction of the new day). The Via Negativa is in the North (the direction from which comes darkness and hard winters, requiring courage) and the Via Transformativa is signified by the West (where the sun sets). In this hoop there is a special relationship between the Via Positiva and the Via Creativa, on the one hand, and between the Via Negativa and the Via Transformativa on the other. If you track the actual journey of the Four Paths within this hoop, you trace a revised "Sign of the Cross," that begins with the body (the South), then moves to the head (the North), then to the East and the West. Earth is first honored in the lower chakra (the tree of the cross was, after all, sustained by the earth), and the Creator is honored by remembering the earth. The liberating Logos is honored in the forehead, and the Spirit of Wisdom is honored in the extremities of East/West.

Paths Two and Four, the Via Negativa and the Via Transformativa, are also related in a special way because we cannot
enter compassion (Path Four) if we have not entered the darkness of suffering and pain (Path Two). Compassion is often
born of a broken heart, and all persons who live fully have
their hearts broken—the dark night of the soul is common to
us all. The struggle for justice is born of the experience of
injustice. When our guts turn over, as they often did for Jesus
(the Greek word used in the gospel to describe Jesus' relationship to those in pain literally means "his bowels turned over"),
passion for justice making and for celebration begin. Path Four
in many respects is a response to the suffering of the world and
of the self that we undergo in Path Two. But by the time we
arrive at Path Four we are more fully equipped—thanks to the
awakened imagination and creativity of Path Three—to respond
to suffering not just with anger but with creative, effective
works that truly heal. In addition, however, the prophetic vocation that lies at the heart of Path Four is not an easy one; in it
we ourselves undergo still more of the Via Negativa as we take
on the sufferings of others in the process of mutual liberation.

If Abraham Heschel is correct when he writes that "man's
[sic] sin is in his failure to live what he is," then it is essential
to *know who we are* as a species. The new creation story helps us
to know who we are, and the Four Paths of creation spirituality
help us *live who we are.* The Four Paths assist us in the telling of
our stories at the level where each of our stories is sacred. Everyone has a sacred story to tell. We are a spiritual species, capable
of relating to all things as beauty. And because we are spiritual,
we are also capable of destroying all things. Being so young a
species on this planet, with immense powers of creativity, we need
ways that help us guide that creative energy in directions that
allow our passion to mature into compassion.

Charlene Spretnak, author of *The Spiritual Dimension of
Green Politics,* tells the story of how her daughter recently
returned from school, where she had been told that the soil was
disappearing because of the way our culture is abusing it.
"Mom, do something," her child demanded, grabbing her arm.

Re-visioning our religious heritage so that it truly honors the
soil as a divine locus and teaches humans the importance of
recovering a mystical relationship to it strikes me as something
well worth doing. We can change our religious rituals so that
they empower us to both appreciate the earth and defend it
creatively against abuse. Such changes in our religious and
spiritual paradigms are a significant step in the redemption of
the earth.

❖ 2 ❖

Gifts of Creation Spirituality

Theologian Leonardo Boff encourages people to meditate on the "avenues of grace" that are available as resources to us. "Where, in our reality, is grace embodied?" he asks. What follows are some gifts or graces that creation spirituality offers us in our time.

A New Cosmic Creation Story

A new cosmic creation story is important because, historically, all tribes have kept themselves together through their creation stories. Today, with scientists agreeing the world over on the basic facts of the new creation story, we have the potential for a sense of global unity, an experience of the human race as a single tribe bound together by a single, amazing, creation story. The ancient tribes of native peoples built their cultures on their creation stories, as did the writers of the Hebrew Bible. And all four of the Gospels of the New Testament begin with creation stories.

What does a creation story do for us? It grounds us in the history of how we arrived here, and it awakens awe and wonder that we are here. When this happens, we are less subject to manipulation, to trivia, to titillating distractions, addictions, and consumerism.* Awe and amazement are the results of a rich creation story, and the awe we feel should encompass our very selves, since every self is part of the unfolding creation

---

*As Anne Wilson Schaef puts it, "The addictive system is largely unaware of potential, gifts, excitement, aliveness, or the extravagance that surrounds us and in which we may take joy. The kind of extravagance I am talking about does not cost a great deal of money. . . . Simply being alive is extravagant!"

27

story. We feel our interconnection with other creatures and
peoples on this surprising planet in this amazing universe of
one trillion galaxies, each with 200 billion stars. One lesson
learned from taking in the creation story is how gratuitous our
existence is. Why do *we* exist and not others who have never
existed and never will? What have we done to merit our existence? Why the unique self that I am and not some other combination of genes or facial features or voice or eye or color or
parents or siblings or place or time of birth or . . . ?

In the context of today's cosmic creation story, these questions take on still more wonder because the nineteen-billion-
year history that has birthed our planet and us is so vast, so
complex, so apparently full of chance and good luck. For example, if the expansion of the original fireball over a 750,000-
year period had been one-millionth of a millionth of a second
slower or faster (or if the overall temperature of the fireball had
been one degree warmer or colder), we would not be here. On
hearing these and other decisions made by the universe itself
on our behalf, we are driven to say, with the fourteenth-century
English mystic Julian of Norwich, that "we have been loved
from before the beginning." Gratitude seems to swell within us.
When persons are full of gratitude, all kinds of creativity come
forth, imaginations are freed, prisoners are liberated, energy is
restored and generosity returns. As Aquinas teaches, "gratitude
gives back more than it has received."

All origins are sacred. To hear stories of our origins that are
fresh and true is to reawaken reverence and awe among us. We
return to our origins in a sacred journey we make together when
we share a common creation story. Recently I had the privilege
of spending three days with forty scientists, social activists, and
artists discussing the new creation story. At the end of the meeting we went around the table evaluating the session. Strange to
tell, at least half the members of the group were struck by how
little competitive "ego" had emerged from this group of many
experts and authors. To me it is clear that when an origin story
becomes the focus of our common endeavors, the ego does not
have to be aggrandized *or* demolished—it finds its proper place.
Because there was so much *reverence* in the room, the ego was

handled in a healthy, cosmological setting. This reverence came from our common focus on our sacred origin story.

The yearning in the human community for a creation story does not emerge solely from a curiosity about our origins. It is also about our destiny. As Thomas Aquinas said, "As the end of a thing corresponds to its beginning, so it is not possible to be ignorant of the end of things if we know their beginning." If the human race can begin to realize a common origin today, then we can also begin to see anew our common destiny and to act accordingly. Our ethics will emerge from our shared origins and our shared destiny—the alpha and omega of our lives. Our source and goal shall emerge together. We shall learn to agree on a "preferential option for the poor" because a creation story instructs us in the fact that in our origins we are all poor, all born naked and dependent on others, all born gratuitously into this vast cosmic dance; not one of us has earned it. When we suffer, if all are not saved, none of us is saved, and the gift cannot go on being given.

An Awakened Mysticism

A second avenue of grace that creation spirituality offers us is an awakened mysticism. People cannot live gracefully or peacefully, joyfully or justly, without celebration in their lives, without awe.*

---

*Einstein defined mysticism as "standing rapt in awe" and Rachel Carson captures the awe we all felt as children when she writes:

A child's world is fresh and new and beautiful, full of wonder and excitement. It is our misfortune that for most of us that clear-eyed vision, that true instinct for what is beautiful and awe-inspiring, is dimmed and even lost before we reach adulthood. If I had influence with the good fairy who is supposed to preside over the christening of all children I should ask that her gift to each child in the world be a sense of wonder so indestructible that it would last throughout life, as an unfailing antidote against the boredom and disenchantments of later years, the sterile preoccupation with things that are artificial, the alienation from the sources of our strength.

(A teacher recently told me she felt that children today lose their mystic child before third grade.)

The etymology of the world *mysticism* is "to enter the mysteries." What the new creation story is telling us all today is that
we are surrounded by mystery: an elm tree that produces six
million leaves every season is a mystery; so are our blood cells,
which parallel the structure of the chloroplasts that make
plants green, except that one atom in the molecular structure
of blood is iron instead of magnesium. Every organ in our
body has a nineteen-billion-year history that makes it a source
of wonder and awe. What is sacred is what is awesome.*

When society lacks awe or mysticism, life becomes trivial-
ized. As Rabbi Heschel put it, "Forfeit your sense of awe, let
your conceit diminish your ability to revere, and the universe
becomes a marketplace for you." After a recent lecture in Palo
Alto, California, a man came up to me and said, "I am a brain
researcher at Stanford University. For twenty years I have been
in a laboratory researching nothing but the right hemisphere
of the brain. I am now ready to publish my work. What I've
learned is that the right hemisphere is all about awe."

The true mystics I have known have been people who never
lost the sense of the child in wonder. The mystic, after all, is the
divine child in us all wanting to play in the universe. A cosmology allows us to find our place in the universe again. Bereft of
a mystical cosmos the past three hundred years, our civilization
has reduced awe to the next anthropocentric invention, resulting in the estrangement of individuals, of the artist, of the
mystic. In isolation we turn to the idolatry of consumerism
wherein buying replaces making. The recovery of the creation
tradition encourages a great mystical awakening in our time.
Joseph Campbell put it this way: "The first function of mythol-
ogy—myths and mystical rituals, sacred songs and ceremonial
dances—is to awaken in the individual a sense of awe, won-

---

*Scientist Beverly Rubick and I recently conducted a ritual wherein we
honored the mystery of our bodies by showing slides of twenty-five bodily
organs and inviting people to chant a response of gratitude for each. Following the ritual, a participant stood up and said, "I have been a drug addict
and an alcoholic and if anyone had led me through this ritual when I was
a teenager, I never would have abused my body the way I have."

der, and participation in the inscrutable mystery of being."
Creation spirituality can reawaken the deep, passionate, and
joyous sense of ritual that human communities require for survival and for instructing one another in healthy living.

Deep Ecumenism

In awakening our capacity for cosmic ritual and for a mysticism
that is more aesthetic than ascetic, creation spirituality promotes a movement among all world religions called deep
ecumenism. This ecumenical movement is based less on theological position papers than on shared mystical practices.
Meeting in sweatlodges, ceremonial dances, and rituals ancient
and new that allow us to experience the awe that we share in
common—this is the heart of deep ecumenism. The implications of this movement are untold, since never before have the
world religions faced one another with such a deep awareness
of our need for mutual wisdom. Given the invitation to ritual
that lies at the core of a new cosmic story, and given the peril
that the earth is facing, our religions dare not fail at sharing
their common wisdom and praying together from the heart.

A New Story of History

A new creation story ingested in the depths of our ritual, myth,
and ceremony is also a new story of history. It places humanity's history within the context of the history of the cosmos
itself. For example, it puts humanity's fratricidal wars into perspective, for it allows us to see the utter relativity of human
ideologies, institutions, nation-states, and religious periods. It
places our human problems into a species perspective and this
allows our imaginations, which are our greatest assets in solv-
ing our problems, greater play. If spirituality can be defined as
a "meeting with God in history," as Leonardo Boff defined it,
and if a new historical epoch is opening, then a new meeting
with God is also upon us, a God that is less warlike and less
patriarchal, more concerned with compassion, justice, celebration, beauty, and creativity.

Creation spirituality does not just invite persons who have been ignored for centuries to be subjects of history; it empowers them to be co-creators of a new historical vision. As Bartolomé de las Casas, who worked on behalf of the native peoples of the Americas in the sixteenth century, put it: "God is the one who always remembers those whom history has forgotten." Mystics and artists, women and sexual minorities, and the *anawim* (those without a voice) are all invited to take their place as subjects of history. In this history, mystic and prophet are nurtured in one and the same individual and community. In this history, an individual hero is not held up for emulation so much as is the entire mystical/prophetic community. Creation spirituality teaches that the human race is entrusted with the history of this planet and the children to come upon it. Therefore, our spiritual and ethical ways of living need to be worthy of the beauty that is to come. All are entrusted with this sense of history; all have their gift to return to the cosmos. Creation spirituality helps heal the division between history and mystery, prophecy and mysticism, social change and personal growth, humanity and creation.

A few years ago I led a day-long retreat at Corrymeela, a peace center in Northern Ireland where Catholics and Protestants come together for healing and rejuvenation. Before going there I met with some Northern Irish for advice, and a very vocal man told me not to go. "We're at war," he said. "We don't want to hear about cosmos and creativity, image making and circle dancing." I went anyway.

The sixty-some persons who arrived at the center for the retreat were exhausted; they looked as if they were carrying twelve years of war upon their shoulders, which indeed they were. I brought out the crayons. We went through the Four Paths of creation spirituality with imaging, shared stories, and discussion. We ended our time together with a spiral dance and other circle dances on the lawn overlooking the ocean. People literally skipped away at the end of the day, and a woman came up to me and said, "This one day has put the last twelve years of our sad history into a totally different perspective."

A totally different perspective—with it, imagination can flow again, and with imagination comes healing. A re-visioning of the history that has preceded us and made us who and what we are occurs when we are given tools to recover the wisdom of the past. For example, Eckhart has been rediscovered by Westerners largely through the creation spirituality movement—not just through translations of his work but through a hermeneutic (that is, an interpretation using the Four Paths) that allows us to live out the depth and humor, the joy and justice making integral to his teaching. Mechtild of Magdeburg, whose life was fully dedicated to serving the poor and young, emerges as an amazing chronicler of the mystical journey that culminates in compassion. Francis of Assisi is rescued from the "bird bath" sentimentalism that has diluted his radical message of simplicity and ecology for so long. And Nicolas of Cusa emerges from obscurity to instruct us in a cosmic view of religion and life. Julian of Norwich and Dante emerge from the shadows of archaic medievaldom to tell us anew about truths like the Cosmic Christ and panentheism and their political implications. Thomas Aquinas, so long interpreted by rationalist "Thomists," can be appreciated as one of Western history's greatest geniuses of cosmology, whose passion for science, psychology, mysticism, and art was insatiable. Creation spirituality re-visions the Bible and asks new, but very ancient, questions of it, honoring as it does the wisdom literature and the ancient tradition of the Cosmic Christ.

This process of re-visioning equips us with powerful tools for understanding our journey today, for exciting the imagination, without which that journey cannot happen, and for re-placing us in the joyful company of a veritable communion of saints. Our ancestors deserve a voice today through us. Creation spirituality allows the best and often most forgotten and repressed elements of our tradition—the shadow side—to come to the fore.

The Return of the Artist

Creation spirituality gifts us by welcoming the artist, who has been cut off from her and his right to community, to serving the community at large, to feeling a part of the whole community. Recent Western history has denigrated the artist and created myths of alienation and isolation, myths about the "beatnik" artist, the alcoholic artist, the "madman" artist. Many of these myths indeed become self-fulfilling prophecies, for artists cannot survive without a living cosmology and few were able to find one in society itself.

The tradition of creation spirituality invites the artist back from the estrangement of the commercialization and secularization of art. I recall leading a workshop on Meister Eckhart's Four Paths in London a few years ago. Afterward, a joyous participant, an actress in the London theater, told me how eager she was that I return and do workshops like that just for theater people. "Our world has become so commercial," she said, "yet we are in the theater because of the spirituality, and there is so little spirituality left."

We do not have an inkling of the power that will be unleashed when artists are welcomed back to education, to religion, to the healing arts, to the service of the people in a cosmological setting. No one can predict what gifts the human imagination has in store for us, for imagination is a thing of mystery, a treasure house of secrets untapped until some genuine invitation comes along to elicit them. The artist names holy "isness" in all its forms—joyful and beautiful, sad and tragic. We need the artist to name our common experience of "isness"— to tell us when "isness" has just passed by and to assist us in expressing our gratitude.

Creation spirituality elicits the artist from every person. This is a dangerous thing, but a necessary and joyful part of all liberation. To experience our own creativity, which invariably involves a return to our origins, constitutes a rebirth of self that holds the key to the rebirth of all society's ailing and tired structures. Robert Fox, a street priest in Harlem for twenty-eight years, used to say that *the only thing outsiders can do for the poorest of the poor is awaken their creativity*. That accomplished, the poor will indeed liberate themselves.

The Recovery of Compassion

Creation spirituality helps us recover the meaning and importance of compassion. "Compassion is the first outburst of
everything God does," says Eckhart, summing up the best of the
spiritual traditions, east and west, north and south. We are
called to compassion when we are called to be "sons and daughters of God," for God *is* "the compassionate One," as the
Hebrew Bible teaches and as Jesus so well understood. Compassion is the essence of Jesus' teaching, and indeed of the
teachings of all great spiritual figures from Mohammed to
Isaiah, from Lao Tzu to Chief Seattle. Yet compassion has been
sentimentalized and severed from its relationship to justice
making and celebration. Creation spirituality resets the jewel
of authentic religious faith within the matrix of compassion.

By doing so, creation spirituality links the struggle for justice with the yearning for mysticism. The community's needs
become the individual's needs and vice versa. Prophecy—the
struggle for justice—and mysticism—the experience of awe, wonder, and delight—form a common dialectic, a tension that in turn
births new possibilities for community and individuals alike.

Creation spirituality also insists not just on justice among
humans but on geo-justice—justice between humans and the
earth and all her creatures. We cannot have authentic human
justice without engaging equally in the struggle for justice
toward our home, the planet earth. There is no need to choose
in an either/or fashion between the human and the nonhuman.
In the struggle for justice, justice toward the rain forest cannot
wait until justice among humans is accomplished. We are too
interdependent for that.

Furthermore, the struggle for the rights of whales and of
the soil, of forests and the air, can so capture the imaginations
of humans who are seemingly apathetic or indifferent to injustice toward humans, that they eventually wake up to injustice
toward the human as well. To enlist ourselves in the struggle for
the liberation of any of God's creation eventually renders us

vulnerable to the struggle for the liberation of all creation. For compassion means, as the mystics have always known and as contemporary science is finding out, that "all things are interdependent," in Eckhart's words, and "all things are penetrated with connectedness," as Hildegard of Bingen said. *Compassion is the working out of our interconnectedness; it is the praxis of interconnectedness.*

The Redemption of Worship

A theology of the Cosmic Christ instructs us in how every creature is a living image of divinity. When the Cosmic Christ is remembered once again, worship can be redeemed. Worship that is dull or boring, overly comfortable or excessively comforting, worship that does not transform and is therefore dead is the result of anthropocentrism. The universe is not boring. There is no atom, no flower, no light beam, no insect, no whale, no human, no star that is boring. Since creation is not boring, why should worship be? We render worship boring only when we leave out creation, when we reduce worship to human dimensions because our souls have shriveled up from too much fear, busyness, or compulsion to control.

Liturgy means "the work of the people," and worship, as Thomas Aquinas taught, is for the people, not for God. If it is not working for the people because the forms are outdated, then the forms must change. Creation spirituality invites us to change the forms we have for worship in the West so that we can give expression to our new cosmology.

The recovery of the ancient tradition of the Cosmic Christ awakens us to the holy presence of the cosmos in worship again. It allows—indeed insists—that our bodies move once again in ritual, that our collective bodies become living rosaries, spiraling galaxies that say something about our journey through the universe. It unites young and old, literate and illiterate, for it invites worshipers to put down their books, take off their glasses, and move in simple circles once again.

Because it invites the child in us and the child among us back to worship, it performs a deeply healing act for the wounded child in all of us, for the oppressed child in our culture, for the yearning in all comfortable adults to *let go*.

When science, mysticism, and art come together again, our worship will delight, amaze, allure, and empower us. We will be healed in these settings, because the Cosmic Christ heals. I have never performed rituals—whether on the windswept fields of New Zealand or in a large hall at Fort Mason in San Francisco—when outsiders did not stop what they were doing to observe and, if possible, join in. Young boys park their bicycles, adolescents put away their skateboards, old men put their noses against the glass windows to peer in when creation spirituality rituals are happening. Humans are a liturgical species. Like other animals, we cannot live without ritual.

An End to Shame

Creation spirituality offers an avenue of grace by sounding an end to internalized oppression, shame, and self-hatred. We are not here to bemoan our existence, to blame ourselves or others, or to wallow in our sinfulness. Rather, we are here to return blessing for blessing and to give our gift back to the larger community. Otto Rank defines the artist as one who "wants to give back a gift," and he understands all neurosis to be the result of the failed artist, the *artiste manque,* in every person. We are whole and healthy only when we create

Creation spirituality promotes healing because it enlarges the heart. The English word (from the French) for "heart-enlargement" is *courage.* Courage is the sine qua non of the virtues, for with it anything can happen, but without it only puny things occur. An increase in imagination often results in an increase in courage, for we get stuck when we see no way out of the fear, shame, or self-hatred that imprison us. Awakening the imagination awakens the heart and stretches it.

The Prevention and Cure of Addiction

Creation spirituality provides medicine that both prevents and cures addiction. It gets to the heart of the addictive pattern of behavior because it gets persons in touch with their feelings once again. Much drug taking is an effort to dull feelings of emptiness. As Anne Wilson Schaef puts it, "The addictive system encourages addictions to keep people far away from their feelings and awareness so that they cannot challenge the system." In that system, Schaef writes, "We are trained not to be ourselves. We lose touch with ourselves. We reference ourselves externally." In contrast to the external referencing that goes on in addictive processes, the mystic Meister Eckhart advises: "Become aware of what is in you. Announce it, pronounce it, produce it, and give birth to it."

Mysticism is by definition an opening up to cosmic wonder and cosmic pain. The Via Creativa cuts through this emptiness and empowers us to be true to ourselves, to let the "true self" be expressed in word, color, dance, and work of all kinds. It is precisely through the Via Creativa that we are empowered to "be ourselves" and to "reference" ourselves "from the inside out," as Eckhart put it. The Via Creativa then spills into the Via Transformativa where we do indeed challenge the system and offer alternatives to social apathy and injustice.

The Celebration of the Young

Creation spirituality graces the youth because it celebrates the worth of the young, the nineteen-billion-year yearning of the universe for the unique existence of each new being. All tribes of humans have passed on their creation story in order to inspire their youth to great things, to the cosmic adventure that birthed them and that calls them to continue the process. Youth need a vision and have a right to it. Creation spirituality provides a vision in its renewal of worship and its renewal of education, where room is made for the magnitude of each individual soul set in the sparkling context of the cosmos itself. With creativity, discipline is learned, and discipline is a friend to youth because it assists them in coming into their own, in growing up and out without losing touch with their unique and truest self.

In addition, creation spirituality honors the youth in every person by combating "adultism"—the tendency to horde things for the older ones, those in power, those with money and access to the decision-making apparatuses of society. Creation spirituality, which celebrates the divine child who is the *puer* in every adult, thus invites adults to let go and become young again. When adults can do this, the young prosper, for communication between generations becomes a matter of mutuality and not an issue of paternalism and dependency. And adults can appreciate the young instead of resenting them.

Creation spirituality defends the young to the extent that it defends the health of mother earth, her water, soil, forests, air, and creatures. When creation spirituality offers effective resistance to those who would despoil the earth by enlisting adults in an effort to defend mother earth, the young are given hope. For it is they and their descendants who will suffer most if the earth they inherit is desecrated.

Letting Go

Creation spirituality offers an avenue of grace by encouraging people to let go and by teaching that the process of letting go is both necessary and generative. Creativity is preceded by receptivity and emptying. The fact that letting go is at the heart of spiritual growth is good news for both overdeveloped and underdeveloped peoples. The fact that some people have too much, while others have too little, are related. There is no way to restore balance to the relationship of "First" and "Third" worlds without the "First World" learning to let go. For example, as John Robbins points out in *Diet for a New America,* if North Americans were to cut their meat consumption by a mere 10 percent, 60 million human beings could be fed yearly on the amount of land and grain that would be saved. Is there a single North American incapable of this? Letting go is at the heart of spiritual growth and of economic and ecological justice.

In a recent interview farmer/poet Wendell Berry offered yet another example of letting go. Asked how seriously we can take the interest in environmental issues brought about by events like Earth Day, Berry replied, "I don't think we can take it seriously until people begin to talk seriously about lowering the standard of living. When people begin to see affluence, economic growth, unrestrained economic behavior as the enemies of the environment, then we can take it seriously. But people are saying, 'Give us everything we want *and* a clean environment,' and this isn't a possibility."*

In the Gospel of Matthew, letting go—repentance—precedes justice. We have to let go (follow Path Two) before we can do justice (Path Four). For the overdeveloped world, letting go allows us to cease denying and accept the truth. But it does not have to be a matter of sackcloth and ashes. Letting go can be done in celebrations and rituals that allow us to grieve and

---

*Or, to take still another example, consider "Third World" debt. The "First World" demands payments on a huge debt owed by the "Third World." Latin America owes the United States, Japanese, and European banks $380 billion. (To put this in perspective, the U.S. spends $380 billion on the military alone in 1.3 years.) Each year Latin America is expected to pay $70 billion in interest to "First World" banks with no payment on principal. This indebtedness is just the latest expression of colonialism and servitude that began when the first colonizers from Europe shipped gold and silver of the Americas back to Europe and enslaved the Indians. In the sixteenth century fierce debates raged in Europe over the question of whether America's native peoples had souls or not—that is, whether they were human. Today this racism is being played out by the silence that dominates the North American news and educational system regarding the history of the struggle of Latin American peoples and the shameful role of North American intervention there. This silence renders the "First World" ignorant, and that ignorance allows us to collude in politics by rhetoric and demagoguery and allows for military interventions in "Third World" countries.

that also inspire us for the next stage of relationship. Imagine, for example, the rituals that could develop around letting go of $100 billion of our defense department budget in favor of investing in truly defending our future by way of toxic clean-ups, good schools for our young, rehabilitation for drug addicts, health care for the needy, housing for the homeless, and good work for the unemployed.

Empowerment for an Ecological Age

Creation spirituality empowers us for an ecological era, a time when we cease looking *up* for divinity and start looking *around*. (It is telling that the word *environment* comes from the French word *environ*, meaning "around.") A panentheistic spirituality—a spirituality in which we see "all things in God and God in all things," as Mechtild of Magdeburg wrote—tells us to look around for the divine who is found both in the glory and in the real pain of our times. When Jesus preached that the reign of God was *among* us, he preached about a panentheistic relation-ship to divinity. Our capacity to experience the divine all around is mysticism.

Ecology means the study of our household. What we are learning from the gift of a new creation story today is that our household, the earth, is a very special accomplishment of the universe. A greater ecological awareness teaches us how endan-gered this household is. From a cosmology we also learn that our shared home is not only this amazing planet but the entire universe of one trillion interdependent galaxies. Thus, all ecol-ogy must be placed in the context of cosmology.

In the twelfth century, the philosopher Adelard of Bath made the observation that if humans cannot get to know the "admirable beauty" of the cosmos, then they deserve to be cast out of it, just as a visitor in a home who is oblivious to the hospitality being offered him or her deserves to be expelled from the home. We are experiencing that reality today, and future life on this planet is gravely jeopardized.

Rabbi Heschel taught that there are three ways humans can respond to creation. "We may exploit it, we may enjoy it, we may accept it with awe." To accept with awe—the way of the creation tradition—would mean a complete *metanoia* (or conversion) for Western civilization. The gifts of creation spirituality can help bring about that change.

3

Gifts of Wisdom:
Rules for Living in the Universe

To be able to call the universe home again is a great blessing. For too long Westerners have been alienated from the universe, stuck in our human-centered world. The new cosmic story can help us overcome that alienation. Awe and delight return. The psalmist wrote, "We get drunk on the beauty of thy house" (which Aquinas glosses as "the universe"). The universe is indeed a source of intoxication, but like any other source of inebriation, it requires discipline lest we be overcome by its power. These disciplines amount to rules for living, some of which I discuss below. These rules name the responsibility we need to take for living in this home.

The aboriginals of Australia, the most ancient tribe on the planet, say that "our Dreamtime teaches us the rules for living in the environment."* The idea that morality and ethics are derived from our knowledge of the universe is common to all wisdom teachings. Rabbi Heschel says that "awe is the beginning of wisdom" and "praise precedes faith." Wisdom is about living harmoniously in the universe, which is itself a place of order and justice that triumphs over chaos and employs chance for its ultimate purposes.

---

*"Dreamtime" includes the time of creation and co-creation, the time of the communion of the saints and of realized eschatology—the fullness of time experienced as the reign of God here and now.

Extravagance

Annie Dillard writes about this rule when she says, "If the landscape reveals one certainty, it is that the extravagant gesture is the very stuff of creation." She continues:

> Nature is, above all, profligate. Don't believe them
> when they tell you how economical and thrifty
> nature is, whose leaves return to the soil. Wouldn't it
> be cheaper to leave them on the tree in the first
> place? This deciduous business alone is a radical
> scheme, the brainchild of a deranged manic-depressive
> with limitless capital. Extravagance! Nature will try
> anything once.... This is a spendthrift economy;
> though nothing is lost, all is spent.

I cannot read this passage without thinking of the Native American tradition of the "give-away." Nature gives away things, a lot of them, extravagantly. For example, all the energy that the sun transmits to our planet represents one billionth of all the energy that the sun gives out! Yes, nature is extravagant—but are we? Thomas Aquinas taught that when people have the necessities for living and more than that, they have an obligation to give away the rest to those who lack the necessities and that if they do not, those in dire need have the right to take what is necessary for their survival, an act that "is not, strictly speaking, theft."

Extravagance is also translated into ethics when humans are challenged to be openhanded, bighearted, and large souled.*

---

*Aquinas speaks of the virtue of magnanimity, the opposite of pusillanimity: "Now everything has a natural inclination to accomplish an action that is commensurate with its power: as is evident in all natural things, whether animate or inanimate." When humans withdraw from their power, they commit a sin of pusillanimity, which "makes a person fall short of what is proportionate to his or her power, by refusing to tend to that which is commensurate thereto." Aqunias feels that pusillanimity—the burying of our talents—is a greater sin than presumption, "since thereby a person withdraws from good things." There is more danger in our remaining small and thus depriving others of our gifts than in offering those gifts and thus tempting pride, ambition, or envy. Sins of omission are grave sins; they multiply when we lose the cosmic spirit of extravagance.

Do we, with souls as large as the universe, "spend all" the way the universe does? Or do we hoard our very souls themselves and die unspent, untapped, and disengaged?

Interconnectivity

Interconnectivity is now understood as a basic law (or "habit," to use scientist Rupert Sheldrake's term) in our universe. A supernova explosion birthed every element in our bodies. The molecules of blood in our bodies are identical to the chlorophyll in green plants save for an atom of iron substituting for an atom of magnesium. The gravity that has me sitting in my chair is also moving planets and galaxies in the farthest distance of the universe, one trillion galaxies away. Spend ten minutes in a room with others and you are all breathing in one another's water vapor—breathe deeply and you are inhaling at least one molecule of air that Jesus breathed on earth, or Mary or Mohammed or Abigail Adams or. . . .

Today's science tells many stories, and they are all about interconnectivity. But how does this translate into a moral law for humans? Thomas Merton provided the answer when he wrote that "the whole idea of compassion is based on a keen awareness of the interdependence of all these living things, which are all part of one another and all involved in one another." Compassion is the moral law of interconnectivity, the cosmic law of responding to another's pain and suffering as well as to another's joy and celebration.

Expansion

Ernesto Cardenal writes that "the greatest discovery of the twentieth century is the expanding universe." But while the universe is expanding, are we? If not, we are contracting. Where there is fear, writes Aquinas, contraction takes over. Fear "denotes avoidance in general," he teaches; to allow fear to take over our ways of living or our hearts or our institutions is to void a cosmic law: the need to expand through love and courage.

The fundamentalism that rules so much religious consciousness today represents a failure of love, a failure to enlarge the size of our hearts. So too do all expressions of racism, sexism, classism, adultism, sectarianism. These are examples of the human species settling for contraction when the universe is urging us to expansion. Persons and institutions stuck in fear oppose the universe as they attempt to build bigger moats and thicker walls of defense or develop more orthodox litmus tests. It takes a lot of energy to fight the universe itself—energy that could be used for more productive tasks.

To celebrate and enter into expansion is not to deny that contraction also occurs in the universe. Limits are important. For example, a painter limits the size of her painting by a conscious decision about its form, and then she pours herself out into that form in as fully expansive a way as possible. Or consider our lungs. If they only expanded and never contracted, we would explode.

But the general message of the universe is: "When in doubt, expand." As Jesus and other moral teachers have told us, "Love has no limits." Love expands to the breaking point and beyond—in other words, to crucifixion and then on to resurrection. The breaking point, the end point that Jesus experienced in his crucifixion, was not the end of the story. The belief in resurrection carries us beyond intimidation, which fear and contraction preach, to the world of divine surprises that, like the universe itself, are beyond our wildest imaginations.

Variety

The universe celebrates diversity and variety. I remember snorkeling off a Pacific island once, where I encountered more colors and varieties of shapes and forms of fish than I could have ever imagined. How many other revelations of the universe's commitment to variety are yet to be encountered by humanity?

The invention of sexuality, about 1.2 billion years ago, ushered in an unprecedented celebration of diversity. For it is through our inheritance of DNA in sexual reproduction that each of the traits of our ancestors gets shaken up, like colors in a kaleidoscope, and spilled out into infinitely new varieties and possibilities. Thanks to sexuality, as cosmologist Erich Jantsch points out, an "extraordinary genetic variety" was made possible and a unique acceleration of evolution occurred, resulting in an "explosion" of life forms. Novelty abounds as a result of sexual transfer. Individuation deepens and develops. The acceptance of variety and diversity and the celebration of both are key to our fitting into the universe.

Creativity

The universe is nothing if not creative. How different a law this is from Newton's conception of the universe as a machine, when, as Rupert Sheldrake put it, "there was no freedom or spontaneity anywhere in nature. Everything had already been perfectly designed." We now know that from the first millisecond of the Fireball about nineteen billion years ago, the universe has been teeming with creativity. Birthing, begetting, dying, and being born—all this happens to stars and planets, to galaxies and microbes, to plants, birds, animals, and humans. Indeed, the human has inherited some apparently unique powers of creativity—unique in their capacity for the demonic and the destructive. (What other species has found it necessary to invent the Trident submarine or to consciously destroy the rain forests?) Creativity in the human is where the divine and the demonic meet.

We need to understand our creativity within a cosmic context in order to diffuse some of it and to discipline all of it toward goals of compassion, justice, and harmony. Creativity is the human giving birth as the whole cosmos does and as God does. It is our godly power at work. "What does God do all day long?" Eckhart asks. "He/She gives birth." So does the universe, and so do its healthy citizens, among whom we humans can and ought to be included.

Emptiness

Emptiness, nothingness, spaciousness are everywhere in the universe: black holes, empty wombs, hollowed spaces. An atom is empty space wherein fields of energy can dance. The universe is a macrocosm of the same dance hall. Things are *solitudinous*. We humans also need our solitude. Our bodies alone are 99 percent empty space; all atoms are. How about our minds? Healthy mysticism praises acts of letting go, of being emptied, of getting in touch with the space inside and expanding this until it merges with the space outside. Space meeting space; empty pouring into empty. Births happen from that encounter with emptiness, nothingness. Solitude is built into nature itself. We need our space in which to dance our dance. Let us not fight emptiness and nothingness, but allow it to penetrate us even as we penetrate it.

Justice

Justice, the quest for balance and symmetry, for equilibrium and dialectic, for homeostasis, is integral to the universe. No wonder Aquinas teaches that justice is the most important of the virtues. Injustice is a rupture in the universe, an affront to cosmic wholeness, an invitation to chaos, an unraveling of the ropes that bind the universe as a whole. It is by justice that we bring together the broken, neglected, cut-off, impoverished parts of the universe to render them whole again.

Beauty

Ernesto Cardenal says that we can argue about the reason for the universe and the meaning of the universe but not about the *beauty* of the universe. Annie Dillard comments that "unless all ages and races . . . have been deluded by the same mass hypnotist (who?), there seems to be such a thing as beauty, a grace wholly gratuitous." We all share beauty. It strikes us indiscriminately. It may be when our child was born into this world; or a simple flower; or a song; or a smile on a face; or a great act of courage; or a dance well done; or a child's laugh; or a loaf of bread baking; or finding a worthy job; or a snowfall; or laughter between friends; or the death of a loved one returning to his or her Source. There is no end to beauty for the person who is aware. Even the cracks between the sidewalk contain geometric patterns of amazing beauty. If we take pictures of them and blow up the photographs, we realize we walk on beauty every day, even when things seem ugly around us. The Navajo people have a prayer that deserves to be sung daily by all persons:

> I walk with beauty before me
> I walk with beauty behind me
> I walk with beauty above me
> I walk with beauty below me
> I walk with beauty all around me
> Your world is so beautiful, Oh God.

Because beauty is a habit of the universe, it is essential that humans be about the good work of showering one another with beauty, and of bringing out the beauty of one another. Not to do this is to obstruct the universe's intention. Injustice, it seems to me, is always ugly. What is just is beautiful and brings back the beautiful to what was broken. All works of healing are works of making beauty, and all beauty heals. The composer Gustav Mahler said that our sole obligation in life "is to be as beautiful as we can in every way. For ugliness is an insult to the beautiful God."

Community

Things live and thrive in communities. Ecosystems are communities. The relationship of chloroplasts and mitochondria, which produce oxygen for all living things, is a cooperative relationship about which biologist Lewis Thomas observes "there is something intrinsically good-natured about all symbiotic relations necessarily, but this one, which is probably the

most ancient and most firmly established of all, seems especially equable. There is nothing resembling predations, and no
pretense of an adversary stance on either side." Competition is
not so much the law of the universe as is cooperation in community. Writes Thomas, "There is a tendency for living things
to join up, establish linkages, live inside each other, return to
earlier arrangements, get along, whenever possible. This is the
way of the world."

Humans are thus invited by the universe to join this "way of
the world" and to build community as well. We cannot live or
grow without community, yet we try, especially in our Western
civilization. All community is first *base* community—that is,
small and local, where all members are invited to express themselves, to experience intimacy. Yet in a world of interdependence, we also learn how community extends to the furthest
shores of our imaginations. We are connected to the stars and
supernovas even as we go about our tasks of serving food to
one another on this planet. The cosmic and the local interact
in community, and in community we learn the both/and les-
sons of living. In community we learn that survival does not
belong to the "fittest" (understood as being the "toughest"). Survival is about learning how to fit into our community and how
the community fits us.

Sacrifice

One law in the universe seems to dictate that things eat and get
eaten, are born and die for the sake of other generations of
evolutionary surprises. Annie Dillard comments, after watch-
ing a "giant water bug" swallow a frog whole, "That it's rough
out there and chancy is no surprise. Every live thing is a sur-
vivor on a kind of extended emergency bivouac." Erich Jantsch
comments on this phenomenon as well: "With the possible
exception of photosynthesizing plants, all life lives off other
life—and we still do, even if we do not devour our prey in the

open fields, but employ slaughterhouses and specialists for the preparation of our food." Even if one has forgone the habit of eating meat, we still kill plants in order to eat. The universe is indeed busy eating and being eaten. Jantsch gives the example of how huge colonies of red mangroves generate conditions of life for other plants, but in doing so, the mangroves become extinct. He calls this an "unselfish way" of living on the part of these trees and concludes from this and other examples in nature that "the ultimate principle of evolution does not seem to be adaptation, but transformation and the creative diversi- fication of evolution. Similar to the death of individuals, the death of whole species in ecosystems, too, furthers evolution."

Is not this "law of sacrifice" part of religion's contribution to human awareness? In Christianity, we might call this law the "Eucharistic Law of the Universe"—a law that teaches that transformation and sacrifice, eating and being eaten, applies to divinity itself. We eat the divine every time we eat bread or anything else; we drink the divine every time we drink wine or anything else. All eating and being eaten is a reverential and awesome act, for we are imbibing nineteen billion years of his- tory every time we eat anything, and we are ingesting divinity itself when we eat. We too will be food one day for other gener- ations of living things, so we might as well begin today by let- ting go of hoarding and entering the chain of beings as food for one another.

Sacrifice requires a response of gratitude. In fact, the word *eucharist* means "thanks." I say "thank you" for the orange that died for me this morning when I drink a glass of orange juice by promising to be as succulent and round and radiant as an orange throughout the day.

Suffering and Resurrection

All suffering may well be sacrificial suffering, a gift of our very being for others. Jesus taught that "greater love than this no one has, than to lay down one's life for a friend." Whole species have been called upon to lay down their lives for others, and they have done so. Supernovas die amid a great act of birthing new life. Leaves die just after their most glorious moment of color, and they are recycled as nourishment for the tree's progeny. Dying and being reborn, crucifixion and resurrection, are not the anthropocentric events we might have thought. Or, to put it differently, the paschal mystery that Christians celebrate in the life, death, and resurrection of Jesus is in fact the celebration of a cosmic law: all things live, die, and are transformed. There is hope in this law, and mystery too. Those of us who are alive to reflect on these things do not know what the dying process promises us, and so we "enter the mysteries," the ritualistic events that name this great cosmic cycle of things. Perhaps the Easter event ought not to have surprised people as much as it did. Perhaps Jesus' being raised from the dead is what divinity does to all it creates. Perhaps, after all, no beauty is lost in the universe.

Paradox and Humor

I sense that the cosmos is not only full of surprises, but also full of jokes. Do all creatures play the role, unwittingly of course, of cosmic comics? Are we here to amuse one another as well as the gods and goddesses, the visible and the invisible? Do the angels laugh at us just as we laugh at them? If life becomes death and death becomes life, and darkness turns into light and light into unbelievable darkness—are there any limits to the amount of jesting that goes on in the universe or the number of surprises that stun us?

To attempt to live without humor, without awareness of paradox all around us and within us, without the ability to laugh even and especially at ourselves is to contradict the universe itself. Too much sobriety violates the laws of nature. What Eckhart calls "unself-consciousness" is often expressed in our ability to let go with cosmic laughter; it is a necessary dimension to common survival and therefore to our ethics. Erich Jantsch writes that "openness to novelty" is part of an evolving consciousness.

One person I know who dedicated his life to naming the paradoxes of existence was Ken Feit, who called himself a "spiritual fool." He challenged persons to attempt to listen to "the sound of clouds bumping or a car clearing its throat or grass growing or a leaf changing color." One of his favorite acts was to liberate ice cubes:

Did you ever liberate an ice cube?
An ice cube, after all, is water that's kept in prison
to serve humans' needs by cooling their drinks
and soothing their headaches.
Well, I sometimes ransom bags of ice cubes
from gas stations,
take them to nearby ponds, and let them go
so they can return
to their water brothers and sisters.

Is Ken Feit being foolish? Or wise? And what is he bringing out of us by his wisdom, or foolishness, or both? I believe the universe holds the answer.

Work

When I look at the universe, I find that all creatures are busy doing work save one. The planets are doing their work, the sun is doing its work, the galaxies seem to be doing their work, the trees are doing theirs, the earthworms and soil, the rocks and the forests are doing theirs. The dolphins and the whales, the sharks and the elephants, the ants and the spiders all seem to be about their work. Only the human seems at times unemployed. I wonder why it is that we humans have invented unemployment and, along with it, the crime, despair, self-hatred, and poverty of spirit that often accompany it. Unemployment is an affront to the universe, an intolerable sin of our species. Why have we invented it when there is so much good work that needs to be carried out—work of putting others to work, of educating one another about our place in the universe and therefore of our capacity for play and art and our powers of healing? We exist to work and enjoy and to stir others to work and enjoyment, as Goethe once wrote. When we do good work, we make the "cosmic wheel go around," Hildegard said.

We might come to the conclusion that the "rules of living in the universe" discussed here are more than rules: they are virtues, sources of strength and empowerment. We shouldn't be afraid of power; used correctly, we need it. Mechtild of Magdeburg celebrates authentic power when she says, "Power is made for service. I am your servant; I am not your master. Be a servant. Not a master." In these thirteen ways of wisdom lie authentic empowerment—ways to serve the universe.

❖ 4 ❖

Cosmology, Liberation, and Wisdom:
A Holy Trinity

At a recent lecture at a university in Australia a man asked, "I have heard you speak of the Cosmic Christ, of cosmology and mysticism, but are you a Christian? Do you believe that Jesus is Lord and Savior, or don't you?" I replied, "I am a trinitarian Christian. Those who think that Christianity is exclusively about Jesus are in fact heretics. They deny the trinitarian divinity."

Because a trinitarian divinity unleashes much power in our imaginations, it can heal or redeem us in this critical time of the planet's life. "Jesusolatry" is not only a heresy but a distraction from the issues at hand. It contributes to the ongoing sins of omission on the part of churches that refuse to see the radical nature of the demands being made on us all. Classical Christian theology, as Martin Luther pointed out, is guided by three basic articles of faith: creation, redemption, and sanctification. In many respects, these articles parallel the persons of the Trinity: the Creator, parent God; Jesus the Liberator; the Holy Spirit who sanctifies. To zero in only on redemption from sin is anthropocentric and leaves out the mystical experience we have of God in creation and of the Spirit in our world. It leaves out the Cosmic Christ, the Cosmic wisdom that is present even before the creation of the world (Prov. 8:30) and who is incarnated in Jesus (John 1:14) and whom Jesus promises to send as Spirit (John 14:26, 16:13). Cosmic wisdom, we are told, "makes all things new" (Wisd. of Sol. 7:27 and Rev. 21:5); she "makes friends of God and prophets" and "deploys her strength from one end of the world to the other, ordering all things for good." She "works everywhere" and is "designer of all" (Wisd. of

55

Sol. 8:1, 5, 6). To emphasize "redemption" as a kind of litmus test for religion is to ignore creation (the Creator) and sanctification (the Spirit). It kills mysticism because it aborts cosmology.

It is not just Jesus who loves us. The Creator and the Spirit also love creation. Eckhart teaches that our very generativity comes from our dwelling in the Trinity in a panentheistic way— the whole Trinity creates when we create! The Creator of the earth—and not only the Jesus of history—needs to be reverenced today. The Spirit that came at Pentecost to teach all nations to end their altercations around the Tower of Babel needs to be welcomed and experienced. This is the same Spirit who breaks through in the mystical awakening common to all religions and to all artists, lovers, and others in the communion of saints. When the mystic is liberated, the Trinity is allowed its freedom. The divine imagination emerges once again, and the mystic becomes an agent of liberation, a prophet.

The number three is a sacred number signifying many things. Among them are the idea of spiritual synthesis, the solution to conflicts posed by dualisms, childbirth, and the yes—no dialectic to life that expresses the mystical—prophetic tension of living in the world. The trinitarian way of seeing the world is rich and hums with energy. I would like to present one trinitarian symbol that I sense coming together in our time—the Holy Trinity of Cosmology, Liberation, and Wisdom.

The First Person: Creator of the Cosmos

Why do I refer to Cosmology, Liberation, Wisdom as a "Holy Trinity"? Consider that the universe reveals God the Creator. The Creator is the one who fills the cosmos everywhere with beauty and power, light and darkness in an ongoing act of creation. Cosmology is the human effort to understand and enter the cosmos by way of science, mysticism, and art: by way of *science*, because science gives us the story of the cosmos unfolding, including its unfolding into our own species; by way of *mysticism*, because mysticism is the awe we experience at being citizens of the cosmos, who did not make ourselves or our habitat but were welcomed here with unconditional love; and by way of *art*, because through art we respond with gratitude to the awe by taking responsibility for expressing ourselves as cosmic citizens.

Consider also that God the Creator is the "Face behind all faces" (Nicolas of Cusa) in the cosmos, the one who made all beings, who is present in all beings, each of whom is "like a mirror, glistening and glittering" with the divine visage (Hildegard of Bingen). God is the Subject behind the subjects that science studies. And God is the Mind behind the human mind that studies the truth of the universe—indeed the mind of the universe. God the Creator is also the Beloved One to whom the mystic responds—the Awe behind the awe. God is the Creator of the human heart with all its potential for cosmic delight and cosmic suffering. God the Creator is the Heart behind the heart that is opened by awe and by suffering to infinite compassion. God's is the heart broken to be made more cosmic, more grand, more magnanimous whenever a human heart undergoes its expansion.

God the Creator is also the Artist of artists, the "supreme artisan [who] made the universe like a great zither upon which he placed strings to yield a variety of sounds," as Honorius of Autun wrote in the twelfth century. God the Creator is the supreme artist, the Art behind the art, the Imagination behind all imagination. The human is the image of God the Creator and therefore is radically creative, relating image to Image, beauty to Beauty, truth to Truth in the One Creator—Artisan of all being. All "isness" is holy (God is "isness," says Eckhart). All this pertains to the God of Cosmology, the first person of the Trinity.

The Second Person: The Logos of Liberation

Now consider how God as Divine Child, the second person of the Trinity, is richly named by the movement of liberation. God is the Liberator. Such a God in human form is a prophet, as Jesus pronounced himself to be early in Luke's Gospel:

The spirit of the Lord has been given to me,
for God has anointed me,
has sent me to bring good news to the poor,
to proclaim liberty to captives
and to the blind new sight,
to set the downtrodden free,
to proclaim the Lord's year of favor. (Luke 4:18ff)

Jesus as prophet—God, as liberator—God, inspires, moves, teaches, and graces all persons as prophets. The divinity in us breaks through not only as creators and co-creators but especially as prophets who interfere with injustice while proclaiming freedom for the downtrodden. How interesting that the passage from the prophet Isaiah cited by Jesus in the temple speaks of being "anointed by the Spirit of the Lord" (Isa. 8:23–9:1), for the word "Christ" means the "anointed one." Jesus the Liberator has become the Cosmic Christ and lives in each one of us who are anointed as prophets after his death and resurrection to bring "good news to the poor."*

The poor to whom we are sent today are the children and grandchildren to come. They are poor if the earth they will inherit is diminished in its health and beauty. Among the poor are the rain forests and the seas, the soil and the air, the winged creatures and the finned ones, the four-legged and the two-

---

*Jesus is also a unique incarnation of God in history both as Logos (the Word) *and* as Wisdom. An increasing number of biblical scholars are rediscovering the Sophia tradition in the New Testament, a tradition that became subordinate to Logos texts under pressure from early Gnostic movements in the church. Paul speaks of Christ as Sophia (1 Cor. 2:7, 15:23, 26, 51; Rom. 16:25). As Susan Cady, et al., indicate in their study of Sophia, "the secret presence of Sophia in all things is the basis of Paul's understanding of the new creation . . . and resurrection of all in Jesus" (see 1 Cor. 5:17). In the prologue to the Gospel of John, the name "Logos" is substituted for Sophia; Jesus is Sophia in John's Gospel. In the Gospel of Matthew, Jesus is presented, in O'Connor's words, as "wisdom incarnate," and in Luke's Gospel, Jesus is also proclaimed as Sophia on numerous occasions (see Matt. 11:25–30, 16:19, 23:34–40; Luke 7:31–35, 10:21ff, 11:49–51, 13:34ff). Jesus' use of parables throughout the gospels is itself a form of wisdon literature.

legged. We are all dying at the hands of our own species. Together we are growing very, very impoverished. God, as child, the "word made flesh," the "perfect image of God," has called us God's "sons and daughters" and in that One we are a "New Creation." Thus, the second person of the Trinity anoints us as liberators. As with the suffering servant of Isaiah, there will be a certain price to pay for our labors on behalf of justice.

Jesus is also a rabbi who liberates by his teachings. Among them are the Beatitudes, which can be understood anew in light of the Four Paths of creation spirituality. The entire motif of the Beatitudes is a restoration to original blessing; "Blessed are you," Jesus promises with each beatitude. We here have a "definition" of salvation as the restoration of each one of us to our original blessing.

Blessing is primary in Jesus' mind—how to recover it, experience it, and pass it on in the human sphere. In these Beatitudes the second phrase is always a promise. Jesus offers a deep psychology of how we change people: people are transformed by hope, by promises of what will be blessing to them. The appeal is entirely to the Via Positiva. If we line up all Jesus' promises as they appear in his Beatitudes, we are promised that we shall

> have the reign of heaven,
> inherit the earth,
> be comforted,
> be satisfied regarding our thirst for justice,
> be shown compassion,
> see God,
> be called sons and daughters of God,
> possess the reign of heaven,
> rejoice and be glad.

Who could resist such blessings as these? Notice how maternal and nurturing these promises are. They appeal to us so deeply because we lack them so intensely.

If we return to each beatitude we learn the lesson of how to experience the blessings that are promised.

1. "Blessed are the poor in spirit, for theirs is the reign of God." The reign of God is ours *now*—but only to the extent that we are "poor in spirit": simple, open, eager to wonder, to dance, to play, to let go. That is, to the extent that we are unself-conscious and in touch with our own mysticism. The "now" contains the reign of God; truly awe and delight are ours. Jesus begins with the Via Positiva.

2. "Blessed are the lowly, for they shall have the earth for their heritage." We *have* the earth if we are in touch with the earth, if we are close to the earth—earthy—and thereby lowly and gentle. Like the reign of God in the first beatitude, the earth is sacred and present now. For those who have eyes and hearts to see, the earth is the locus of the reign of God. What limits our experience of the earth, however, is our underdeveloped *receptivity,* so the second beatitude introduces the Via Negativa as a source of increase for the Via Positiva. To be "lowly" is to let go.

3. "Happy are those who mourn; they shall be comforted." Here too Jesus names the Via Negativa, the need to enter the darkness, taste the pain, undergo the grief. Here too he hints at the Via Creativa, for all grieving comes from inside out and is a kind of art as meditation: we give birth to our grief. But life does not consist of pain alone; there shall be comfort too, limits to the grieving.

4. "Happy are those who hunger and thirst for what is right, for they shall be satisfied." Like the previous beatitude, this one promises satisfaction if the hunger and thirst are truly felt. Struggle is implied in the terms "hunger and thirst"; to be hungry and thirsty is to be in the Via Negativa, to be emptied and at a loss, "to sink," as Eckhart describes it. But the hunger and thirst in the Via Negativa are what urge us on to the Via Creativa and the Via Transformativa; passion leads to compassion.

5. "Blessed are the compassionate, for they shall have compassion shown them." Compassion is mutual; it is catching—others get it from you and you get it from them. Compassion

is the culmination of the New Law. How best do we experience compassion from others? By practicing compassion ourselves! The Via Transformativa depends on the Via Creativa. If we give birth to compassion in our creativity, morality, and choice making (the Via Creativa), we will share it in the Via Transformativa.

6. "Blessed are the pure of heart, for they shall see God." This beatitude parallels the previous one. Compassion leads to purity of heart. To see God is to be shown compassion, for God is the Compassionate One. Seeing God is the culmination of the spiritual journey, the best of the Via Transformativa. How do we see God? By being simple, nondevious, straightforward, childlike, and wonder filled. "By our deeds of justice," Eckhart says, "we make God dance for joy."

7. "Blessed are the peacemakers, for they shall be called sons and daughters of God." We become "sons and daughters of God" by being peacemakers, justice doers, prophets. *All* are called to be prophets, for in our hands lies the responsibility for economics, justice, and good work. Peace requires justice, so a peacemaker is a transformer of hearts and social structures that stand for injustice.

8. "Blessed are those who are persecuted in the cause of right: theirs is the reign of heaven." The prophetic task is not a pleasant one—it conjures up the shadow side of individuals and institutions afraid of their own liberation. The Via Transformativa does not come about without struggle.

9. "Blessed are you when people abuse you and persecute you and speak all kinds of calumny against you on my account. Rejoice and be glad, for your reward will be great in heaven. This is how they persecuted the prophets before you." Part of the Via Transformativa is realizing that we share in the communion of saints. All saints have struggled to bring about transformation.

Jesus celebrates the Via Creativa and its relationship to the Via Positiva when he declares: "You are the salt of the earth.

But if salt becomes tasteless, what can make it salty again? It is good for nothing and can only be thrown out to be trampled underfoot. You are the light of the world. A city built on a hill-top cannot be hidden. No one lights a lamp to put it under a tub; they put it on the lampstand where it shines for everyone in the house. In the same way your light must shine in the sight of all so that, seeing your good works, they may give praise to your Creator in heaven" (Matt. 5:3–16). Light is the first gift of creation, and the Cosmic Christ is the "light of the world" (John 8:12). So too the light (Via Positiva) that we make shine before others (through the Via Creativa) awakens still more praise in the universe. To refuse to give birth is to squelch the light that is our unique gift; it is to choose darkness, therefore, and to let shadows rule.

The Third Person: The Spirit of Sophia

Wisdom can be understood to correspond to the third person of the Trinity, the Holy Spirit, the fecund spirit, the spirit of generativity, the spirit who broods over the fetal waters of birth, of transformation and of Pentecost, the spirit of the elements of the universe, the cosmic spirit of all nations of the earth.

The spirit of divine imagination, the spirit of all truth who continues to bring us the truth we have not yet heard, the spirit who unites us all in deep prayer and spiritual praxis, the spirit who sustains us in persecution and injustice, the spirit who is "ever green" (Hildegard) and who is the "trans-former" (Eckhart) is essentially a feminine spirit. The spirit who maintains our greening power, our wetness and fertility (who begot Isaac in Sarah's belly after she was too old to bear children; who begot Jesus in Mary's belly without manly help; who can and will beget new images, new forms, new social and psychic structures in all of us who feel a part of civilization that is by all outward appearances too old to begin anew); the spirit of the New Creation; the spirit open to all, especially the poor, those at the bottom, on the margins, at the point where nothingness meets despair and darkness overwhelms—this is a feminist spirit. This passion for nurturing at all costs, for birthing in spite of all odds, for embracing the whole and not settling for the part, for dancing in the cosmos and not just in the man-made rooms of our psyches and institutions is at the heart of authentic feminism.

This is the dream that mysticism is just as important as prophecy and that "peace and justice kiss" (Ps. 85:10). Eros is as integral to justice making as it is to life itself, and life will renew itself with or without us. Erotic justice insists that we join the river of life, the wet movement of all living things, the fertile crescents of our land and our moons, the tides of our oceans and of our cities and our bodies—join them all, dive in, for the spirit knows no boundaries and will never be quenched or drowned, "for love is as mighty as death, passion as fierce as the grave; its flames are a blazing fire. Deep waters cannot quench love, no flood can sweep it away" (Song of Songs 8:6–7).

This spirit of eros and of pathos cries out still through the suffering creatures of our time, through the suffering children of God, for wisdom, for Sophia. Enough knowledge, enough computers, enough information, enough studies undertaken. Give us wisdom! Mother Sophia, Mother Wisdom, come to us! Come through us! Break through us, open our eyes. Set your tent among us.

An Undivided Unity:
God as the Self-Organizing Mind of the Universe

Sophia is being awakened in our time through the new thinking of science. Scientist Erich Jantsch provocatively concludes his book, *The Self-Organizing Universe,* with the statement that "God is . . . the mind of the universe." Jantsch defines "mind" as "self-organization dynamics at many levels, as a dynamics which itself evolves. In this respect, all natural history is also history of mind." Jantsch comments on how the new paradigm of self-organization in science compares to the experience of mystics over the ages: "This connectedness of our own life processes with the dynamics of an all-embracing universe has so far been accessible only to mystic experience. In the synthesis, it becomes part of science which in this way comes closer to life."

I cannot listen to language about God as mind of the universe and the mystical experience of an "all-embracing universe" without thinking of the mystical and cosmological tradition of Sophia or Wisdom. In the biblical literature this mind is personified as a woman who undergirds and "permeates" all things. She brings order from chaos and plays with God from before the ages. She is the object of intellectual pursuit but also the fruit of awe and wonder. She alone satisfies, for she "intoxicates people with her fruits; she fills their whole house with their heart's desire" (Eccles. 1:16). In her is found rest, delight, joy, and the source of all eros—"whoever loves her loves life" (Eccles. 4:12). Hers is the way of justice and authentic law—a law that defends the poor instead of upholding the powerful. She lies at the heart of the creative process, a cocreator of the ongoing process of the universe. It is Sophia who teaches holy ways of living in the universe; she is the matrix for all three persons of the Trinity for she is present as Creator, as Prophet, and as Spirit making all things new.

Consider how this Holy Trinity of Cosmology, Liberation, and Wisdom is interconnected, just as is the universe and the Trinity of classical theology. While separate, the persons are connected: the third person comes through the relationship of the first and the second persons. There can be no Wisdom, no return to Sophia without the interaction of Cosmology and Liberation. With their interaction, wisdom can flow again. The resurrection of the feminine, known both as the "Assumption" and the "return of the Goddess," can and will happen for our salvation, our wholeness.

While the teaching of the Trinity in the Western church emphasizes the outflowing of the Spirit from the interaction of Creator and Child, the Eastern teaching emphasizes that all began with Wisdom. The Holy Spirit, Mother Sophia, was present "before the mountains were settled, before the hills were formed" (Prov. 8:25) and was indeed the spirit "hovering over the waters" prior to creation itself (Gen. 1:21). Thus, the feminine face of God is present in Cosmology itself. The divine feminine is also present in the history of Liberation: Wisdom not only makes all things new, she also "makes friends of God and prophets, deploying her strength from one end of the earth to the other, ordering all things for good" (Wisd. of Sol. 7:27, 8:1).

PART TWO

GIFTS OF LIBERATION

❖ 5 ❖

Establishing the Context

A Costa Rican professor recently contacted me about a statement I had made suggesting that creation spirituality is a liberation theology for "First World" peoples. He said, "You must develop this notion. The vision of 'Third World' liberation theology will be stymied until you 'First Worlders' do your share of liberating and being liberated."

I have long felt that the interdependence between north and south does indeed require a conversion at both ends of the economic/political seesaw, for we are all on this planet together, affecting one another as surely as two partners on a seesaw do. My Costa Rican friend shared a vision he experienced in which the continents of the Americas were a single body: the head in North America, the body in South America, and the heart in Central America. The heart has been hemorrhaging during the past ten years with Contra wars in Nicaragua, civil war in El Salvador, and genocide in Guatemala. The mystical body that is the Americas is sadly diseased. The body is too "top-heavy," too weighted toward North American agendas and systems—economic, political, and military. The body needs liberating from top to toe.

Another urge for exploring "First World" liberation comes from a question that has been so obvious to me over the years that I somewhat hesitate to ask it: "Why is liberation theology and the quest for justice and compassion not immensely more popular than it is in our country?" In other words, if the quest for justice is inherent in every creature—a thesis I laid out in

The Coming of the Cosmic Christ and for which considerable
scientific evidence exists today—why aren't North Americans
and other "First Worlders" more involved in the struggle?

The answer lies in the fact that critical thinking is required
to apply the values of liberation theology to a "First World"
cultural context and this need has not yet been adequately
addressed. You cannot transfer liberation theology from a
"Third World" context to the "First World" and call it liberation. It might be called ideology; it might be called instruction;
it might encourage guilt or shame or some limited action.
But it cannot serve a liberation *movement;* it will not do the job,
for it lacks incarnational roots. Translation is required—not
just of the Spanish or Portuguese words about liberation, but
concerning the historical and cultural context in which persons and their institutions find themselves, about how to
change people, how to ignite their self-interest, and so on. The
fact is that within liberation theologies emanating from the
"Third World" we have varied kinds—some from South Africa,
some from Asia, some from Peru, Chile, Brazil, Central America.

"First Worlders" can no longer escape doing their *home*-
work, which means seeking to liberate our own people and
structures that are, in fact, such a menace to "Third World"
peoples' efforts at liberation. While institutional criticism is
certainly called for, much change must come from within individuals' psyches and ways of perceiving the world. We actually
fail in one of liberation theology's basic principles: to respect
the *context* within which one must practice, and to reflect on the
process that liberation always entails. A failure to respect the
context will result in an ineffective pedagogy for awakening
people to their own liberation. No group can liberate another
group. People liberate themselves.

Why have not more "First Worlders" been interested in
their own liberation? Our own slavery is hidden from us. We
often internalize our own oppression and fall victim to addictions. We need ways to learn the truth about ourselves and our
history, and we need to learn ways of letting go. Leonardo and
Clodovis Boff observe in *Introducing Liberation Theology* that the

great majority of Latin Americans are both poor and Christian. The situation for North Americans (or Europeans, for that matter) is totally different, of course. They are not poor, and the attempt to teach them in the same manner used for the poor of the southern hemisphere is to invite disaster. The bishops of Brazil have stood by the base community movement and the liberation theologians in their struggles with religious and political bureaucracies. But rare is the North American bishop who can be counted on to stand by the base communities, for instance, of Womenchurch or Dignity or Creation Spirituality when they come under fire from right-wing pressure groups in the society or the church. How many bishops took a public stand even when one of their own—Archbishop Hunthausen of Seattle—was being crucified by church authorities in Rome?

Another example of differing contexts for the "First World" and the "Third World" would be the issue of drugs. Basically, the "First World" buys while the "Third World" sells. The "First World" creates the demand, and the "Third World" offers the supply. We cannot, therefore, solve the drug problem by focusing exclusively on the "Third World," as if it were the cause of the problem. The "First World" pathos that leads to drug compulsions must be addressed from within the psyches and structures of "First Worlders" who need to understand why their culture is so desperately in need of drugs. Why is it, for example, that the United States, which comprises 2 percent of the world's population, is currently using 60 percent of the world's illicit drugs? The buyer must be liberated as well as the seller.

Part 2 of this book is not about liberation movements taking place elsewhere—from the "Third World" movements in Latin America, Africa, and Asia, to the recent, astonishing efforts to introduce democratic reforms into the so-called "Second World" of the Soviet Union. This part, indeed this book, is about the need for a liberation movement in the "First World." How do we liberate the "First World" and thereby link up with other liberation movements around the world, not out of romantic nostalgia or left-wing ideology but from a realistic vision and a deep solidarity? Can the "First World" match the courage and passion of the liberation movements of the "Second" and "Third" worlds?

To that end, the next chapter will analyze how creation spirituality might assist in "First World" liberation and in the chapter following that, I will explore how that liberation might be named as an Exodus event in our times. Chapter 8 will explore a consequence of North American liberation and a new solidarity of spirituality between the people of the Americas, both north and south.

✦ 6 ✦

Can Creation Spirituality Liberate "First World" Peoples?

From my experience conducting workshops and giving lectures around the world it is increasingly clear to me that creation spirituality liberates people because it affirms them in their processes of liberation and affirms that they are not alone on their journey. Creation spirituality helps end the isolation of the mystic-prophet that our culture has fostered.

But that is not the only kind of liberation that creation spirituality offers. In *Church: Charism and Power,* Leonardo Boff names several characteristics of liberation theology, all of which can usefully be analyzed in relationship to creation spirituality.

Praxis and Theory

The basic methodology of liberation theology is to insist that theology is to be practiced inductively: that is, theory must grow out of reflection on lived experience, on our concrete historical and social realities. Our experience represents the work of the Spirit in the history of the people, the history of creation. About the various theologies that have emerged from Europe since Vatican II, Boff comments that "new thoughts have produced but other new thoughts. There is no significant break with the past, no substantial move in the direction to a new way of being Christian and being church, no articulation of theory with practices aiming at the transformation of society, and within society practices aimed at the transformation of

73

the Church." What is unique about the methodology that liberation theology provides is its being, in Boff's words, "a faith
reflection originating and developing within the actual practice of liberation."

It is essential to remember that *spirituality is praxis,* the
praxis of religion. So much of religion in overdeveloped countries is in books, buildings, academic institutions, degrees, ser-
mons, and words. While learning is certainly essential to
healthy religion, it is no substitute for praxis. *Thinking* about
God is no substitute for *tasting* God, and *talking* about God is
no substitute for giving people ways of *experiencing* God. "Civil"
or institutional religion can go on with little spiritual practice
but eventually church attendance declines as people begin to
find church less meaningful and less interesting than the entertainment that secular society provides.* Fewer and fewer persons are attracted to Christianity in the "First World" countries
because there is so little practice, so little spirituality in
religion.

Creation spirituality expresses a methodology of "praxis
and theory" through body prayer, art as meditation, the revision
of our mystical heritage, an analysis of our cultural situation,
the appropriation of scientific perspectives, ways of re-imaging
our relationship to divinity, such as panentheism and the
Cosmic Christ tradition, and concrete activities on behalf of
social justice. All of this has one goal: personal and social transformation. All of this emphasizes experience over institution.
Participation flows from persons themselves, not from ossified
and often sterile forms. Creation spirituality, therefore, can
revivify religion and liberate religion from itself. As Jung once

------

*Church attendance of West Europeans has truly tumbled in the past
twenty years: today 7 percent of German Catholics, 13 percent of Belgian
Catholics, 15 percent of Dutch Catholics, and less than 6 percent of Italian
or French Catholics attend Sunday Mass. In England, 3 percent of Angli-
cans practice, and in Scandinavia, 2 percent of Lutherans practice. In the
United States, church attendance is also dropping dramatically among all
except fundamentalist or evangelical church bodies, and it is especially rare
to see young persons attending Sunday services.

wrote, "Only the mystic brings what is creative to religion it-self." What is needed in overdeveloped peoples is a liberation of the mystic. When mystics start gathering together again in worship, the young and the alienated will return, for there is nothing so natural to the human heart than the desire to give thanks. Once the wounds are healed so that people can feel awe and wonder again, the yearning for occasions to praise and give thanks will flow along with the opportunities for effective compassion.

From the *praxis* of those in touch with the mystical journey, creation spirituality has developed a *theory* of the journey. This articulation of the journey is laid out in the Four Paths, which form a spiral along which we constantly dance and expand into ever-larger orbits of spiraling. There seems to be no end to the practical applications of these Paths: with them we can reenter the world of food, of soil, of parenting, of sexuality—in short, the entire experience of living and creating. Over the years, many persons have told me that *Original Blessing*, my systematic exposition of creation spirituality, "names my experience." The result of such naming is that mysticism is honored, celebrated, and encouraged once again. When the Spirit is allowed to flow, our religious traditions are reanimated.

The naming of the journey is part of the methodology in liberation theology. In 1968, the congress of Latin American bishops at Medellín distinguished three stages in the journey of liberation theology. The first is called the "moment of seeing," followed by the "moment of judgment," and finally the "moment of action" in which courses of pastoral activity are charted. Boff writes, "The decisive moment is that of a trans-forming activity: a transforming praxis, in a concrete engage-ment with groups constituted for reflection and action." Notice how these three steps parallel the Four Paths. For to "see" is what occurs in Paths One and Two: to behold the beauty and the darkness without judgment. In Path Three, the Via Creativa, we judge and make a choice of which images to trust, to throw ourselves into; it is the decision-making path along the jour-ney. Path Four, the Via Tranformativa, constitutes the decisive moment of action, of returning to society with the energy and creativity of the previous three Paths to contribute to societal celebration and justice making.

Going beyond mere "thinking" to action based on critical reflection and creative choices, both creation spirituality and liberation theology require praxis and theory.

Indignation

Boff names a second characteristic of liberation theology as the personal and communitarian starting point for that movement, namely indignation. Liberation theology, he writes, "begins with indignation at the poverty experienced by God's children, a poverty that God surely does not will. At the same time, this poverty is seen as a religious experience for the poor in whom the Suffering Servant is present." To experience the poor as the Suffering Servant (see Isa. 53) is also to experience the Cosmic Christ in the suffering ones, the Christ crucified all over again.

There is also indignation experienced at the poverty within overdeveloped nations and peoples. First, of course, there are the materially poor in the "First World." My own country houses immense pockets of poverty that rival the worst found in "Third" and even "Fourth" world countries, except for the immediate *possibilities* of improvement.

Consider the following facts about life in the United States today:

- Twenty million citizens, of whom twelve million are children, will go hungry sometime this month.
- Three to seven million people are homeless, including many who are working families. Forty percent of these homeless are families with children. Fifty percent of the homeless are Vietnam veterans.
- Eight million renters are eligible for low-income housing in a system that provides only 4.2 million affordable units.
- Thirty-six million people lack basic health care.

- Seventy-two million people (a third of the United States adult population) have not completed high school, and thirty-one million adults are functionally illiterate.
- One out of every five children under the age of six is poor.
- One out of every two black children is poor.
- Two out of every five Hispanic children are poor.
- Between 1980 and 1984, the richest 20 percent of American families gained $25 billion in income, and the poorest 20 percent lost $6 billion.
- In 1968 the poorest 20 percent of American families had an estimated 91 percent of the income they needed for basic requirements; by 1983 they had only 60 percent.
- Since 1977, the pretax income of the lower 60 percent of American taxpayers, adjusted for inflation, has declined 14 percent. Yet taxes on this group have increased by $19 billion. In the same period, the pretax income of the top 1 percent of all Americans, with inflation adjustments, has soared 86 percent to an average of $549,000.

Poverty is a growing fact in the United States. The rich are getting richer and the poor poorer. But we don't need to consult statistical tables to see this—it's enough just to take a look at the streets of our cities, with their swelling ranks of homeless and jobless persons and the numbers of families at soup kitchens and drop-in centers. As Barbara Ehrenreich puts it, our society "has succeeded in reducing large numbers of the American poor to the condition of their 'Third World' counterparts—beggars, vagrants, and dwellers in makeshift shelters."

During the eighties, what Ehrenreich has called a "massive upward distribution of wealth" occurred in America: the middle class has also gotten poorer—even when both spouses worked —and is paying more taxes. Accompanying this has been resentment toward the poor who seem to get something for nothing by living on welfare, for example. Yet the poor are the natural allies of the middle class, for the middle class differs from them, for the most part, by virtue only of their education. Furthermore, the vast majority of the ancestors of European Americans did not come from privileged classes in Europe but arrived as victims of joblessness, homelessness, and political and religious persecution. These common roots ought to make the poor and the middle class allies rather than competitors.

Clearly, the "First World," like the "Third World," needs to undergo its righteous indignation, its moral outrage, at the unnecessary fact of poverty and at the despair and violence that it produces. The indignation is real, because God does not will this suffering; indeed, God is undergoing the suffering, for God is one of the poor, the Cosmic Christ within each person crucified again. Any liberation theology for "First World" peoples will have to address the apathy, the loss of indignation, the lack of moral outrage that seems so prevalent in our cultures. (Rabbi Heschel believed, in fact, that ours is a "generation that has lost the capacity for outrage.")

Creation spirituality offers both a theory about why there is so little indignation in the "First World" and a practice by which to reawaken it. Leonardo and Clodovis Boff distinguish between two kinds of poverty: the poverty of the "actually poor" who lack the means to sustain their lives and the poverty of the "evangelically poor," those who leave their places of comfort in order to "establish solidarity with the economically poor and even identify with them, just as the historical Jesus did."

But a third kind of poverty is found in the "First World"— the *spiritual impoverishment* that is palpable where consumerism reigns and materialism runs peoples' lives; where the young are rendered bored or violent to self and others.*

---

*In speaking of this *poverty of soul,* I am not spiritualizing poverty. In fact, poverty of soul and poverty of economic fact are closely allied insofar as a spiritually alive culture would generate the imagination and the daring to deal with the poverty of economic fact. As Leonardo Boff puts it, "There is a causal relationship between wealth and poverty. . . . [There are] mechanisms that produce the wealth of some and the poverty of others." The issue is not to fight the persons who are rich, "but the socioeconomic mechanisms that make the rich wealthy at the expense of the poor."

Among those suffering from this poverty of soul in the overdeveloped world are those who are subject to boredom ("luxury living produces boredom," Hildegard of Bingen observed eight centuries ago) and those who are subject to despair (which comes from being "cut off from one's own divinity," Thomas Aquinas commented seven centuries ago). Joanna Macy, drawing on the experience of conducting workshops on "Despair in the Nuclear Age" around the world, has learned that what passes for apathy in the "First World" is in fact a coverup of despair. The key to ending apathy is to tackle despair, which you do by reminding people of their connection to divinity, their capacity to create and co-create. Others who suffer from a poverty of soul are subject to addictions to drugs, alcohol, work, shopping, food, television, entertainment, sports, religion, nationalism, and fascism. All who succumb to these various enslavements are in a radical sense poor. If this poverty goes unabated, they pass their misery onto their children through violent behavior and through institutional structures that condone violence.

Then there is the growing poverty of Mother Earth. Just as the conquistadores centuries ago laid waste to the indigenous peoples of the Americas, so too the whole world—led by "First World" corporations—is today laying waste to nature itself. The rape and pillage of the earth is expressing itself everywhere in topsoil depletion, water and air pollution, forest poisonings and extinctions, and the extermination of whole species of plants, animals, and birds at unprecedented rates—as well as in the growing malnutrition and disease among human beings, especially the young, that results from this carnage of the earth.*

Not only is the earth being laid waste, but the biosphere that surrounds the earth is also under attack: the hole in the

---

*Current policies in the U.S. Department of Agriculture actually reward those farmers who perpetuate a chemically dependent agriculture and punish those who practice sustainable agriculture and crop rotation, for instance. (Could it be possible that some of the penchant that North Americans have for drugs comes from the fact that the food we eat is so chemically dependent? Does culture not follow agriculture?)

ozone layer over Antarctica (and which is as large as a continent) is a warning that our ways of industry and transportation, of emitting carbon dioxide into the atmosphere, must change. This is especially incumbent upon overdeveloped countries because they produce far more carbon dioxide emissions than underdeveloped nations. It also means that the latter must not imitate the path of the former but must find their own healthier life-style. While I was in Brazil, I was pleased to learn that many Brazilian cars run on forms of alcohol that are far cleaner than the gasoline-driven automobiles of the north.

If, as I believe, health means wealth then the earth is indeed becoming an increasingly impoverished place as we lay waste to its rich blessings of earth, air, fire, and water. Where is our indignation amid all this suffering of the poor?* Any liberation movement must possess the power to awaken moral indignation among its citizens for within that indignation lies the power to liberate.

With only a little imagination and letting go, look what we might do:

- For the cost of two fighter aircraft ($45 million) we could install 300,000 hand pumps in "Third World" villages to give access to safe drinking water.
- For the cost of one Trident submarine ($1.4 billion) we could inaugurate a five-year program for universal child immunization against six deadly diseases, thus preventing a million deaths a year.

---

*The lack of imagination toward poverty in our own culture is reflected in our denial of the facts about poverty in the world at large. Consider the following statistics: 800 million persons live in absolute poverty, unable to meet minimal needs; 777 million do not get enough food for an active working life; 10 million babies are born malnourished every year; 14 million children die of hunger-related causes each year; 1300 million persons lack safe drinking water; 100 million have no shelter; 500 million suffer from iron-deficiency anemia; and 880 million adults cannot read or write.

- For the cost of one nuclear weapons test ($12 million),
  we could train 40,000 community health workers in the
  "Third World."
- For the cost of "Star Wars" ($3.9 billion) we could pro-
  vide elementary school education for 1.4 million children in Latin America.
- Community workers in the Philippines have devised a
  way of creating grassroots work that requires a $500
  investment per job. Using that method, the United
  States alone, by retiring its $300 billion military budget,
  could create 600 million jobs worldwide.

"Investigation of the Ways"

A third dimension to liberation theology is what Leonardo Boff
calls the "investigation of the ways that produce such wanton
misery on one side and scandalous wealth on the other." Here,
historical, sociological, political, and economic analyses are
brought to play so that these socioanalytic tools, read with the
eyes of faith and theology, might discern the "paths of sin."
Among both the factual poor and the spiritually poor in
America, drug, alcohol, and other addictions play an ever more
prominent role. (It has been estimated, for example, that 80 percent of crime in America is drug-related, as is the enormous
increase in the prison population.) An analysis of the drug boom
in the United States must include both a psychospiritual critique
of *why* persons become dependent on drugs as well as an understanding of how drug dealing fills the gap in a poverty-ridden
culture that is looking for employment and money.

For example, we must remember that African Americans
came to America in slave ships. Slavery was a system that
deliberately tore the family apart in order to control its members. The struggle to preserve a family in today's ghetto—where
55 percent of young men are unemployed—cannot be understood apart from this historical and sociological fact. Our capitalist system, which advertises its wares to all classes by way of

television, has not worked for the ghetto dweller, where
between 1973 and 1986, according to George Miller, the number of black males ages 18 to 29 outside the labor market more
than doubled. Over the past two decades, the number of inner-
city ghettos in the United States has also more than doubled,
and crime, especially the drug trade, has taken the place of
legitimate employment. The role of the destruction of the
black family, inherited from the era of slavery, cannot be
underestimated when we attempt to analyze, from a sociological and historical perspective, the rising crime rate, the drug
trafficking, and the bloated prison populations.

Now consider a psychospiritual analysis of what lies behind
the drug traffic in America. The drug trade may produce
employment for the poor, but it could not thrive without the
addiction of the comfortable classes. When it comes to addiction, the poor and the wealthy share a mutual dependence.

In *When Society Becomes an Addict,* Anne Wilson Schaef
defines addiction as "any process over which we are powerless.
It takes control of us, causing us to do and think things that are
inconsistent with our personal values and leading us to
become progressively more compulsive and obsessive." What
does the addictive process result in? According to Schaef, an
addiction "keeps us unaware of what is going on inside us. We
do not have to deal with our anger, pain, depression, confu-
sion, or even our joy and love, because we do not feel them or
we feel them only vaguely." Schaef maintains that "in time, this
lack of internal awareness deadens our internal process, which
in turn allows us to remain addicted." If we do not choose to
arrest the addiction, "we will die. This dying process does not
happen at only a personal level: it is also systemic to our culture." Indeed, it affects all our relationships, including the institutions that educate us and in which we work and worship.

Creation spirituality strikes at the very jugular of this
pathology of addiction. Instead of "deadening our internal
processes," it awakens them. Instead of settling for the denial of
anger, pain, or depression, it names them as the Via Negativa

experiences that every mystic must necessarily imbibe. Creation spirituality gives us tools for awakening our internal processes and entering the darkness.

The joy and love that become deadened in addictive practices are celebrated as the Via Positiva, to which we all have a right. Indeed, the experience of awe is necessary for trusting the dark. You don't enter a cave without a lantern.

Recently I met a young Jesuit priest in Brazil who has been working with the tribes of the Amazon for two years. When I asked him what he had learned from them, he replied without hesitation, "Joy. They experience more joy in a day than we do in a year. And they don't live as long or have as much as we do." Recently some African Americans who visited Africa for the first time were asked by the Africans there, "Why are you Americans so sad all the time?" Joy is lost when a cosmology is lost. Delight is reduced to the pseudo-pleasures of buying and selling, winning and gossiping, living vicariously in heroes and soap operas. Joy—a gift of the spirit—is the starting point for the spiritual journey.

One dimension to addiction named by Schaef is codependence, which she defines as "addiction to another person or persons and their problems, or to a relationship and its problems." Some of the characteristics of this condition are low self-worth, workaholism, doing whatever it takes to be liked, being good sufferers or Christian martyrs, always being a server or a volunteer, being selfless to the point of exhaustion. Says Schaef: "The disease of codependence is the result of years of training. The Good Christian Martyr is the product of careful grooming." Without this codependence, addictive systems could not endure.

In contrast to codependence, creation spirituality teaches interdependence. It attacks the issue of low self-esteem directly by teaching Original Blessing in preference to a psychology of Original Sin. Instead of promoting martyrdom, it teaches that the Via Positiva is at the heart of why we exist—"God enjoys the Godself in all things," says Eckhart. Creation spirituality teaches that we can and indeed need to live life fully and that asceticism as such can be a kind of distraction from that project.*

Schaef detects four elements in an addictive system. The first is *control.* Control, she points out, gives rise to depression when we fail (which we always do) and to stress, which is a "by-product of the illusion of control." There is a compulsion to "play God" in this effort to always be in control. Indeed the "God of the Addictive System," writes Schaef, is "God the Controller." Creation spirituality addresses this compulsion to control directly by teaching the mystical path of letting go and letting be, the Via Negativa. It draws on mystical practices that lead us into ways of letting go. Have you ever taken part in an Indian sweat? There is no way to control in a sweatlodge. You either let go or pass out.

The second element of an addictive system is *dishonesty.* "Addicts are terrific cons," writes Schaef, and the lying often begins when the addict lies to him- or herself. Once you lie to yourself, "it is then impossible to be honest with others, so addicts engage in lying to the people around them" and then in lying to the world. Behind the lying is an assumption that "if they did get in touch with themselves and reveal themselves, nobody would like them." Lies fit the need for control.

Creation spirituality offers an antidote to this lying: art as meditation. You cannot lie to the clay when you work it, or to your body in dance, or to your heart in meditation. Art as meditation celebrates what is inside everyone. It invites the truth to come from inside out. It encourages everyone to listen to the truth and the images inside—and to trust them and give birth to them, and thus to rake the risk of revealing to others the inner person. Paul, Eckhart, and other mystics talk of the

---

*Or, as Eckhart put it, "Asceticism creates a bigger ego instead of less of one. More self-consciousness instead of less." True delight is about *unself*-consciousness, becoming a child again playing in the universe, just as Divine Wisdom is depicted in proverbs: "Delighting in God day after day, ever at play in God's presence, at play everywhere in the world" (Prov. 8:30–31).

"inner vs. the outer" person; we need ways to get to this inner person, to let the truth of our joy and our woundedness speak. When we practice art as meditation (as opposed to art as product), we put our souls out into the community for acceptance or rejection. The Via Creativa allows what psychologist Alice Miller calls the "true self" to emerge.

The mystics speak of self-knowledge and self-honesty as the key to mysticism. Teresa of Avila and Catherine of Siena especially emphasize this virtue, the latter calling self-knowledge the "cell" for the soul's growth and the former calling it the "basement" for constructing the whole soul as a castle or building. Eckhart says that "all the names which the soul gives God, it receives from the knowledge of itself." If this is true, then we had better name ourselves truthfully, or even God will be distorted along with all the other relationships in our lives.

Schaef defines honesty as a process. Getting honest means "getting in touch with one's feelings and dealing with them no matter what they are." The antidote to dishonesty that creation spirituality offers is the Via Creativa.

Schaef also discusses the "abnormal thinking process," with its "almost exclusive dependence on left-brain functions," that supports the addictive system. That system, she writes, is "founded on the worship of linear, rational, logical thinking. This kind of thinking supports the illusion of control by simplifying the world to such an extent that it seems possible to have control over it." The antidote to this abnormal thinking process is an equal amount of right-brain or mystical thinking. Because creation spirituality elicits the mystic from every person, it offers ways of right-brain education that are effective. When you combine this with the analytical rigor of left-brain work, you have authentic learning.

A third element of the addictive process, according to Schaef, is *denial.* "Denial is the addict's major defense mechanism," she observes. We deny the pain of the unemployed, of the "Third World," of "First World" relationships, of Mother Earth, of youth, of ourselves. I was recently visited by a thirty-nine-year-old friend who told me that during a recent session with a body-therapist he recalled for the first time a memory of being seduced by his aunt when he was seven years old. "For all these years," he said, "my mind has buried that memory inside me, but it was still present in the cells of my body." The body does not lie. Listening to it will reveal truths both pleasant and unpleasant. But they all need to be heard, since the alternative is to waste our creative energies on controlling, repressing, or trying to forget the truth.

Surely the feminist movement is an effort to combat denial and to bring the pain into the open so that it can be dealt with. Like many liberation movements, it functions in part by bringing people together to share their stories. Similarly, when men are invited to tell their stories, they often discover that they too have been victims of a system that has so often rewarded them materially but not spiritually. Eckhart says that "God is the denial of denial"—as long as we indulge in denial, God is for all practical purposes absent. For the addict, as Schaef warns, denial becomes the "normal way of being in the world." Not so for the creation mystic: art as meditation, as a primary prayer form, "denies denial" because in art, in expressing one's deepest memories, feelings, and experiences, denial is not tolerated.

The fourth characteristic of the addictive system is *perfectionism*. Schaef observes that "alcoholics, drug addicts, compulsive overeaters are perfectionists. They are convinced that nothing they do is ever good enough, that they are never good enough, that they don't do as much as they should, and that they can be perfect, if only they figure out how." A shame-based religion, one that begins with original sin, encourages perfectionism. However, discovering that we are each an original blessing in a universe of original blessings might heal this belief that we are never good enough. The terms "life of perfection" and "striving for perfection" that dominated the spiritual literature in the West during the fall/redemption religious era feed this disease called perfectionism.

Schaef writes, "In a system that demands perfection, mistakes are unacceptable." By contrast, the Via Creativa is always about making mistakes and even celebrating and learning to recycle them. From mistakes arise diversity and new possibilities. We often learn what is most important by trial and error. The imagination is ignited by what many would call mistakes. A healthy Via Negativa, one that truly teaches us to let go, also assists us in learning to accept our mistakes and live in an imperfect world. In fact, one thing we learn to let go of is perfectionism itself. We can strive for excellence without being addicted to perfection; the two are not the same thing. Excellence is about being the best and the most beautiful that we can be; perfection presumes an outside norm for what is best, ignoring the subjective, the personal, and the unique.

In this chapter I've tried to address the question of why creation spirituality can be understood as a liberation theology for "First World" peoples. I've drawn parallels between certain categories of liberation theology in South America and creation spirituality in North America, including the requirement that praxis and theory be combined, the role of moral indignation, and the critical investigation of the ways of sin and misery. While we need to respect the contextual differences between "Third World" and "First World" liberation, we can see that the movement to liberate the overdeveloped peoples of the northern hemisphere indeed parallels liberation theology in the south. The north, which is so overdeveloped in our bureaucracies, in our heads, in our addictions, in our capacity for denial, in our fear, in our militarism, in our misuse of the world's resources, remains severely underdeveloped in our imaginations and spirits and indignation. We need to get on with the task of liberating ourselves.

❖ 7 ❖

Liberation *from,* Liberation *to:* An Exodus Story for Overdeveloped Peoples

When God led the Israelites out of their slavery in Egypt the leave taking was called an *exodus.* An exodus is a liberating event, a redemptive movement. But liberation is not only *from* some state of servitude or depression or injustice; it is also *toward* something. In the Israelites' case, the movement was toward the Promised Land, toward freedom, toward autonomy and self-organization, toward fulfillment of the divine promise of a covenant of peace based on justice.

So today, a liberation movement not only invites persons to leave behind what is oppressing them, but to imbibe the new, to drink in the freedom, that is the opposite of oppression. The word "liberation," after all, comes from the Latin word *liberare,* "to set free." When one is oppressed, even one's understanding of freedom can be tainted by the diseased worldview of the oppressor or the oppressive system. A grave danger exists of internalizing that worldview, thus making it one's own. It is useful, therefore, to look briefly at the rhythm of "from" and "to" inherent in the liberation dialectic that creation spirituality offers the overdeveloped peoples of the world. Following are some of the liberating directions that a people who follow the creation spirituality path can expect to undergo.

From the Secularization of Everything to the Resacralization of All Things

The overdeveloped world is characterized by secularization in all areas: sexuality, art, work, information, media, soil, farming, parenting, children, war making, money and the way we spend it, health care, science, education, government, and economics. In the overdeveloped world, even religion is secularized in many respects—not only when it is a big business as in the case of television evangelists, but also whenever it fails to awaken the numinous, the awe, the sacred in us. By its considerable sins of omission, religion succumbs to secularization, by which I mean sucking the awe—that is, the sacred—out of the events of our personal and cultural lives.

Creation spirituality teaches that all things are imbued with the divine light, that every creature is a manifestation of the Cosmic Christ, and that divinity permeates all of reality. All of us believed the world was sacred when we were children, and the creation tradition helps us to recover that experience. Ways of meditation and spiritual practices that awaken the senses to their fullest capacities are well developed in the creation spirituality tradition around the world. Included in these practices are ways to let go of the blockages, the pain, and the woundedness to the mystic child in us all that prevent us from experiencing the world as sacred.

From Boredom and Passivity to Wonder, Creativity, and Empowerment

Where there is luxury there is boredom. Where there is boredom there are violence, drugs, and other forms of addiction meant to dispel the boredom, or transcend it, at least temporarily. Luxury living is not what living is about. *Living* is what living is about! But living takes discipline and letting go and doing with less in a culture that is overdeveloped. It takes a commitment to challenge and adventure, to sacrifice and passion. Awe is the antidote to boredom and creation spirituality awakens the awe of being in this amazing universe and being part of its ongoing creativity. We may need to let go and live simpler lives in order to truly see the wonder of what God and nature have wrought. As Eckhart teaches, "God is not found in the soul by adding anything, but by a process of subtraction." People living the creation spirituality tradition learn how this is so. Subtraction can itself become a kind of awesome game, a playful thing, a ritual whereby everyone wins and no one loses.

A paradox is built into our experience of wonder, as Rabbi Heschel points out:

> Wonder, radical amazement, the state of maladjustment to words and notions, is a prerequisite for an authentic awareness of that which is. . . . Endless wonder is endless tension, a situation in which we are shocked at the inadequacy of our awe, at the weakness of our shock, as well as the state of being asked the ultimate question.

Creation spirituality actually assists in *increasing* the amount of awe that is in the universe. How does it do that? By encouraging creativity. There can be no full spiritual journey by any human individual or society where creativity is lacking. The Via Creativa, as we saw in chapter 2, is the pivotal moment in the creation journey of Four Paths. "We are all meant to be mothers of God," Eckhart declares. We are all here to birth a unique expression of the Cosmic Christ, the divine Child of God in ourselves, our work, our culture. Creativity empowers and there is no antidote to passivity like empowerment. It is not only creation that is awesome, but what humans do with their creation—what singers do with voice and song, what dancers do with the body, what Rilke or Adrienne Rich or other poets do with words and images, what parents do in birthing and raising children—all art is awesome. As surely as a tree or a mountain is nature at work, so is every artist.

The tools of creation spirituality could help us unleash imagination at all levels of society, and put that imagination to the service of celebration, healing and justice making in schools and families, in prisons and churches, in hospitals and hospices, in political parties and economic decision making. Television sets would be turned off and people would be turned on. The streets and neighborhoods would ring with music and dance and laughter; gardens would spring up where people learned to grow their food. Good work would abound! Artists' work would heal people. Children would be happy to be alive again. And our prison populations would decrease instead of increase. Where there is joy—what Thomas Aquinas called "the human's noblest act"—there is no boredom and no passivity. Despair and depression melt and give way to energy and vitality.

From Taking for Granted to Thankfulness

Philosopher Josef Pieper defines the essence of bourgeois living as "taking for granted." It is true that those who live in homes where the water always runs through spigots *take water for granted*. And when people always have money they *take their next meal for granted*. Our lives are filled with assumptions about the universe serving us all the time. This is false thinking. Will it take catastrophes to awaken us to the truth that *all is gift*? An earthquake reminds us that not even the stability of the ground underneath our feet should be taken for granted. Death reminds us that not even breathing itself can be taken for granted. As the forests disappear and the soil and waters become increasingly poisoned, we learn that we cannot take air or water or soil for granted.

One way to learn not to take for granted is to voluntarily do without. This is best done in a ritualized context where the community does without together and supports one another through the difficult process of letting go. For example, go without water for three days. Go without food for five days. Go without meat for two weeks. These are ways to learn to *cease taking for granted.* Every overdeveloped person and culture should undertake these periods of fasting. In doing so we learn the basics of gratitude, for not one of us created the waters or the air or the soil or the foods that we take for granted. Fasting also allows us to identify, at least partially, with those millions of the world's poor who can never take eating a meal or drinking good water for granted.

Gratitude changes our lives. It fills us with energy and vitality. When I was twelve years old, I had polio and could not walk for six months. The doctors could not reassure me that I would ever walk again. As it turned out, I did get my legs back. But I learned a lesson in the process that I have never forgotten: don't take for granted. I had taken my legs for granted, legs that work, legs that run and play ball, legs that take me exactly where I want to go. When my legs returned to me I was filled with gratitude—*not* gratitude for the "miracle" of my legs being healed, but rather gratitude *for having legs at all, legs that work.* I was filled with energy and promised myself that I would not waste my legs for as long as I lived.

From Waste to Recycling

One of the overwhelming sins of the "First World" is that of waste. We are a civilization whose major product is waste, and we appear to be the only species that wastes more than it recycles. What we give back to the universe is often not blessing—it is poisonous and nonrecyclable goods. The petrochemical industry   that industry that was the very first to support a young politician named Adolf Hitler in German politics sixty years ago—has developed plastics and Styrofoam that appear simple and cheap but in fact cannot be disposed of even in five hundred years. Our cities are being inundated by our own refuse. We have no way of dealing with the nuclear waste that has proliferated from military and civilian power plants. This lethal plutonium will "live" for at least another 100,000 years: Joanna Macy suggests that instead of burying this radioactive waste in order to deny it, thus making life intolerable for generations to come, we ought to keep it visible above ground, and build monasteries around it to remind us all of its lethal-ness and our mortality. These "guardian sites" would become holy places of pilgrimage for persons who regard the planet as a sacred trust.

We also waste our youth and their talents and gifts. When hope dies, waste takes over. Whether that waste is expressed in the form of crime or drugs, alcohol or prison, despair or sexual addiction, it is living proof of the depth of waste that haunts our consumer society.

How does a consumer society cease wasting? By restoring relationship to the center of our lives and life-styles. If we con-sidered our relation to generations to come, for example, we would cease giving out plastic bags in grocery stores. Recently I accompanied a friend (who is an extrovert) to a supermarket late at night. The cashier asked her, "Plastic bag or paper?"

She replied in full voice, "Plastic? Plastic won't disappear for 500 years!"

The cashier sheepishly responded, "Our manager tells us to push the plastic because it is cheaper."

My friend replied, again in full voice: "Cheaper? It may be cheaper for him but not for our great, great grandchildren!"

The cashier replied: "I guess we don't consider our great-great-grandchildren very often, do we?"

"No, and that's one of the things wrong with our society, isn't it?" said my friend.

It is time that supermarkets and *all* businesses start factor-ing into their economics not only what is cheaper for them but what is cheaper for the earth and her children. We all pay for waste. If we understood our relationships to soil and water, to our great-great-grandchildren and self, we would waste mini-mally and our imagination would be freed up for the great spiritual act of recycling that constitutes Path Three in the crea-tion spirituality journey. All creativity is an antidote to waste since all creativity *is* recycling. Ask any artist.

The greatest waste of all is the waste of our human gifts for ingenuity, good work, healing, and joy. If "joy is the human's noblest act," then to waste our gift for creating joy it is to squander the noblest potential of our species. But joy is indeed wasted in overdeveloped countries. Joy is at a premium. Wherever people have no work by which to express their nobility, wherever they are homeless and without hope, wherever their talents go undeveloped and unnoticed, waste abounds.

From Tiredness to Youthfulness

I believe that the overdeveloped nations show signs of extreme exhaustion: spiritual, moral, and structural. Our cities appear "exhausted" by the problems weighing in on them. Our churches and synagogues are often places of exhaustion, wherein the most we can receive from any liturgical experience is comfort. I attended Mass in Chicago recently at a celebration for a religious community. Two days later I asked a friend what she derived from the Mass: "Well, I didn't go away angry. It was the first time in years." This is certainly a *minimalist* approach to worship! We now feel grateful if we can attend worship that does not provoke us to anger! Yes, ours is a tired civilization that cannot excite its young, that can offer no employment and little education that helps the young to experience the awe of their existence. A tired civilization is cynical and violent and offers "entertainment" to distract people from their depression or despair. "Bread and circuses" replace the passion for justice and beauty. As I wrote in *The Coming of the Cosmic Christ,* a negative *senex* dominates our overdeveloped world, while our *puer* is so underdeveloped and so sadistically treated.

The practice of creation spirituality brings the *puer*, the mystical child, to life again by liberating creativity itself. As Rabbi Heschel, commenting on the Hasidic mystical tradition in Judaism, wrote: "God is not only the creator of earth and heaven. God is also the One 'who created delight and joy'... Even lowly merriment has its ultimate origin in holiness. The fire of evil can be better fought with flames of ecstasy than through fasting and mortification.... A new prohibition was added [by Hasidism]: 'Thou shalt not be old.'"

From Complacency to Compassion

If Rabbi Heschel is correct, then the practice of creation spirituality can liberate the "First World" from its complacency. And how complacent we are! How we ignore the truth of the pain all around us *and all inside us.* How are we rendered so numb? so forgetful? so full of denial? And what can we do about it? To be complacent means to be self-satisfied. I think that, in a consumer society built on self-satisfaction, the term *self* does not stand for the true self but for the false self, the puny self that seizes more than its share of the pie in an effort to boost its ego and then builds armies at astronomical costs to guard that ill-gotten piece of the pie. Our "selves" need to be expanded into the true self, the full self. Eckhart talks about the "old self" vs. the "new self." The old self, Eckhart says, is the superficial and exterior self but the new self is the deepest self, the innermost and the cosmic self. The true self is the *self-in-relationship to all others,* and the "others" include all our sister and brother creatures and all time and all space. We are selves only in relation to other selves.

Science today is teaching what creation mystics have always taught: the interdependence of all. "Geologian" Thomas Berry rightly accuses our civilization of the disease of *autism:* the moral disease that is the ultimate in complacent self-centeredness, marked by total withdrawal from all that does not correspond to the small self. That is the price the overdeveloped worlds are paying for their runaway anthropocentrism. We never factor into our profiteering the suffering or the rights of other creatures. Part of complacency is *denial.* Anne Wilson Schaef says that the opposite of denial is to "see what you see and know what you know." The practice of creation spirituality can help us overcome denial by engaging in prayer forms that insist we listen to the truth and to our images, thus allowing us to see what we see and know what we know. Eckhart says that "God is the denial of denial, the negation of negation." What good news this is—that we can deny denial and we can negate negation, and that in doing so we liberate God, *who actually comes to be* in the process. What does it mean when we say that God comes to be? It means compassion comes to be. "The best name for God is compassion," Eckhart teaches.

The theory and praxis of creation spirituality can assist us in moving from the false complacency and autism of the small self to the work for compassion that will some day allow all persons and creatures to enjoy the banquet of life together. Compassion—understood as living out our interdependence in celebration and in justice making—is the goal of the creation spiritual journey. Thus, creation spirituality liberates us *from* our complacency *to* our potential as divine agents of compassion. I have always noticed how rare passion was among those whose lives are complacent. Compassion, on the other hand, is a kind of *fire* (Aquinas says compassion is the fire that Jesus came to set on the earth)—it disturbs, it surprises, it ignites, it burns, it sears, and it warms. Compassion incinerates denial; it especially warms and melts cold hearts, cold structures, frozen minds, and self-satisfied life-styles. Those who are touched by compassion have their lives turned upside down. That is not necessarily a bad thing.

From Art for Art's Sake to Art for Earth's Sake

The secularization and commercialization of art in overdeveloped cultures has often reduced the artistic vocation to that of salesmanship for unneeded goods on the one hand, or trivialization by way of self-serving complacency on the other. Nothing in the universe is for its own sake. Compassion means we are all connected and related in some way. The artist finds his or her fulfillment in being a special agent of celebration and justice making, of healing and awe naming. Arts are the least expensive, the most fun, and deepest form of healing that humankind has at its disposal. At the Institute in Culture and Creation Spirituality, we offer a course on "Arts as Healing," and all persons, no matter how deeply wounded, can be helped to see anew by way of the arts. Old persons come alive and pass on their stories to other generations, if invited to do so by an art-healer. Prisoners can get in touch with their story and their power of self-expression through art. The same is true for dying persons in hospices and bored persons in ghettos or persons living with AIDS. Teenagers wrestling with dreams that are inviting them to big things can be helped by poets to explore their dreams. Potter and poet M. C. Richards warns of the artist who is tempted to barter "poetry for power." The artist stays to the artist's path. That is her or his gift to the community. From that spiritual commitment the society is truly awakened and healed, moved from complacency to true empowerment. "Art serves," M. C. Richards declares. Art serves the earth. It serves all creatures. It serves the universe.

Creation spirituality names and celebrates the path of the artist. Creation spirituality challenges the artist in our midst to serve the forces of compassion. It liberates the artist and reconnects the artist to the entire communion of saints, all those artists who have preceded us in their effort to name the beauty and the pathos of life on this planet.

The authentic artist always has something to say that heals the community and denies the denials going on in the community. That is why every prophet is an artist and every true artist is a prophet. Religion can so easily fall into moralizing—always judging this as right or that as wrong—and fail to *behold*, to see, to "be-with." These are the gifts of the artist. Jesus was an artist, a storyteller and parable maker par excellence. He knew how to behold (that is, to hold being up for reverencing), to see, to be-with. Thus, he befriended public sinners but made enemies of the socially righteous and powerful.

Creation spirituality befriends the artist by insisting that there is an artist lurking in every human—that this is the divine core, the Creator's image in every person. Humans are called to co-create: "only the human generates like God does" says Eckhart. Hildegard of Bingen teaches that every human who does good works is "a flowering orchard." How reminiscent of Jesus' promise in John's Gospel: "You will bear fruit that remains" (John 15:16). Creation spirituality does not just theorize about our being co-creators and fellow artists with God; it insists that to enter into art as meditation is the primary prayer form for healthy adults. It is the primary path to cleansing and awakening, to seeing anew and to wholeness. To learn centering by way of clay, dance, ritual making, painting, massage, music, Tai Chi, Aikido, chanting, writing, poetry—all these are indeed deep ways of prayer. In creativity we take in the nineteen-billion-year history of blessing that the Universe has bestowed on us and give it out again in new forms, in ways that have passed through our unique imaginations and times, our unique hands and heads, hearts and voices. As Eckhart put it, "What is truthful cannot come from outside in; it must come from inside out and pass through an inner form." All artists know this, and all persons need to learn it.

From Fundamentalist Fear to Trust of the Cosmos

Is fear not the biggest problem in the world today? Is fear not what makes nation-states spend idolatrous sums on weapons while their people go without shelter, food, health care, and education? Is fear not what sets one religious sect against another, one race against another? Fundamentalism in all its varieties—Christian (Protestant or Catholic), Islamic, Jewish— appears to be based on fear: fear of the universe, fear of science, fear of the loss of self, fear of nothingness and Aquinas observes that "all fear derives from love." To get at fear is to get at the issue of what we truly love. What is it that fundamentalists are loving? Is it the power that certain individuals cherish? Or the privileges? Is it their own pain, if their suffering were not denied but allowed to surface? Is it an entire system that they do not want to let go of because they fear a new worldview, an alternative distribution of power? Is it a wounded child inside that has gone neglected?

It occurred to me in meditating on the Christmas story this past year that if Jesus redeemed humans from anything it was *redemption from fear*. The first word the cosmic messenger or angel says to Mary in Luke's Gospel is: "Fear not." The word "fear" is used 365 times in the Christian scriptures—a reminder every day of the year to move beyond fear. The Messianic texts from Isaiah speak at length about overcoming fear. Jesus taught: "Love your enemies" (Matt. 5:44)—our enemies being whatever strikes fear in us. John's epistle states simply that "love drives out fear" (1 John 4:18). Trust of self, of imagination, of others, and of all creation—here lies the basic meaning of faith in the Gospels and in our own time. To be a person of faith is to be a person of trust. Trust is empowerment. "Go your way, your *trust* has restored you to health," Jesus says (Matt. 9:22). Aquinas taught that fear is a sin, and it was the work of the prophets, according to Rabbi Heschel, "to cast out fear." As a prophet, Jesus' work was to "cast out fear." Are those who claim to follow in his footsteps busy "casting out fear"? A healthy spirituality moves persons beyond fear to courage. No religion based on fear can lay claim to following Jesus.

An insight I had while doing a vision quest this past year was that, according to Native American wisdom, the only way that evil can penetrate the human heart is through the door of *fear.* Prayer is essentially about making the heart strong so that fear cannot penetrate there. Where persons or their institutions operate out of fear rather than out of a centered heart, evil can readily follow.

Along with fear goes sectarianism and parochialism. Fundamentalism sees the world as "we the saved" vs. "the others." Among these others are not only all non-Christians as well as all Christians who are of a different sect. Fear contracts us physically and spiritually. It makes the soul small and defensive. By contrast, creation spirituality talks of *deep ecumenism,* meaning the coming together of the mystical traditions of *all* the world religions. This coming together was not possible before our time perhaps because we were not in close enough proximity to the varied cultures and religions of the world and because our sense of history was distorted and we failed to realize the amazing accomplishments of those ancient faiths that Westerners dismissed as "mere paganism."

There is a real sense in which Christians and others must move *beyond* "paganphobia" today. The word *pagan* is simply

Latin for "country person," and the word *heathen* simply means "one who lives on the heath." Why is there so much invective against "country persons"? Is it not due to the repression of our earthiness and the projection of this hatred onto rural persons, peasants, and others close to the earth? Our overly urbanized theologies easily fall into "paganphobia" when they lack a mystical relationship to the earth. Today, when the earth is in such peril at the onslaught of Western science, technology, and religion, it is especially important to seek the wisdom of ancient mystical practices that were so attuned to the cosmos, to love of the earth, to what one scholar has called "aboriginal mother love." Because creation spirituality helps in practice and in theory to develop the mystic in every person, it assists not the closing down of the religious mind but its opening up. There is a universalism in creation spirituality that is appropriate to our shrinking global civilization.

The practice of creation spirituality can liberate us from fear and fundamentalism because it teaches us to let go. Creation spirituality teaches us ways to relearn trust of the universe, working with today's science, instead of in opposition to it. A cosmology teaches us that authentic fear is, in fact, what we have referred to elsewhere as awe. The "fear of the Lord" spoken about by the psalmist is the awe we feel at being in the universe. The "Lord" is, after all, the one who governs the universe.

When we suffer from other kinds of fear, it must be driven out by prayer, which is the act of expanding our hearts. We can build up courage, which is the antidote to fear. If, as native people teach, evil spirits enter the human heart only through fear, then to pray is to be strong vis-à-vis the powers of fear. Creation spirituality teaches us to develop our creativity as prayer. Through creativity, we can be nourished by the great spirits of our universe and we can tap into the art-spirit that belongs to all of us. When we create, we wrestle with evil spirits of fear and pusillanimity, acedia and sloth. This prayer drives out the legions of fear that would poison our hearts and lock our social systems into institutional fear. In this way we can take back the archetype of the spiritual warrior from the Pentagon.

Creation spirituality moves us to let go of the idolatry of nation-state ideologies because it places our lives and our national priorities in the context of creation itself. No single nation can control the flow of water or the purity of air or the health of the oceans and the rain forests. The blessings of creation demand responsibility on the part of all earth's citizens. Thus the fear that isolates nation-states into ideological rivalry pales before the real struggle of our time, which is not nation against nation, but the temptation of our species to destroy other species and the earth itself. Anthropocentrism bores us. This is why a Rambo film requires the constant blowing up of persons and places to keep the viewer entertained. Violence is the result of a bored culture.

Thomas Aquinas warns of the "sin of fear" and how "those who are in great fear . . . are so intent on their own passion that they pay no attention to the suffering of others." This explains why justice and injustice are not often discussed in fundamentalist religions. When one is constricted by fear one does not see justice and injustice. Fundamentalism does not criticize injustice. I have noticed that the categories of "justice" and "injustice" are not in the vocabulary of fundamentalist preachers. Yet the Scriptures teach that to love is to do justice, and Eckhart says "compassion means justice" and "the person who understands what I say about justice understands everything I have to say."

From an "I Think Therefore I Am" Philosophy to a "Creation Begets Therefore We Are" Philosophy

René Descartes, the French philosopher who lived from 1596 to 1650, has influenced "First World" education and thinking for three centuries. Creation spirituality takes opposite positions on just about all of Descartes' basic principles. For example, Descartes states that the basis of his philosophy is the observation, "I think, therefore I am." Creation spirituality responds: "No! How egocentric and self-conscious a starting point for education and society this is!" Rather, we should say: "Earth exists and therefore we are." Or, "Creation begets and therefore we are." Notice the differences: in creation spirituality the human is spoken of in the plural—we are a species and a race, a community. If the starting point for philosophy is the "I," then we risk that the ending point will also be the "I." Modern civilization is a testimonial to this fact. Notice too that the world does *not* begin with the human but with creation itself, which in fact is what birthed us. Furthermore, the world does not begin with *thinking,* but with birthing, art, and creativity.

A second principle of Descartes is that of the separation of mind and body, spirit and matter. Like Augustine, to whom he is philosophically indebted and who preceded him by twelve centuries, Descartes was a dualist. He saw matter and spirit as antagonistic and irreconcilable. Augustine said "the soul makes war with the body" but Eckhart, representing the creation spirituality tradition, said, "the soul loves the body." Matter in the creation tradition is not an enemy to spirit but is a home for spirit, a place of spiritual power, magic, and élan. In this tradition, spirit finds a home in matter and in psyche as well as in its own right. Descartes writes about controlling nature. He teaches that animals are machines that have no souls, no consciousness—one cannot hurt an animal but only "damage" one. Creation spirituality teaches quite the opposite: that humanity is to *reverence* all beings, which are all examples of divine "isness." We may use nature provided we do so reverently and with respect. We are not to control or dominate nature.

Another philosophical tenet for Descartes was his teaching that truth is primarily "clear and distinct ideas." This definition renders truth an abstraction and divorces it from intuition, from compassion, and from feeling. It tempts an entire civilization to live and learn only from its neck up—as if body, heart, feeling, outrage, and art have nothing to teach us. Descartes' philosophy has no treatment of aesthetics. *Beauty is banished as a philosophical and moral category.*

In contrast, creation spirituality celebrates the whole person—right brain and left brain, body and mind, soul and

spirit (they are not the same thing in a nondualistic philosophy), feeling and judgment. Not only is there a place for passion and compassion, but compassion marks the culmination
of the spiritual journey in creation spirituality. Not only is
beauty of concern to creation spirituality, but those who help
name it for us, the artists, are educators par excellence, for they
are the ones equipped to draw the divine beauty, the Cosmic
Christ, from each of us. Art is the *heart* of the spiritual journey,
the Via Creativa being pivotal to all Four Paths. Descartes
declared that his philosophy would make humans "masters and
owners of nature." He prophesied correctly—up to a point.
Creation spirituality proposes a totally different relationship
to nature than that of mastering and owning it: that of relating
to it interdependently, trusting it, and reverencing it.

Because Descartes' influence has been so overwhelming in
Western education and science, it can truly be said that to
consciously move beyond his thought would constitute a paradigm shift for the West—its professions, education, science,
and self-consciousness. Creation spirituality consciously and
deliberately embarks on this paradigm shift. It seeks to leave
many of Descartes' basic philosophical teachings behind in
favor of more ancient teachings. One might name this paradigm shift as moving from *I think therefore I am* to *Creation begets,
therefore we are.*

From Theism to Mystical Panentheism

One way in which fear is legitimized in us and our institutions
is through the images of God that we carry about with us. Theism teaches that God is outside us and usually "up there," at the
top of the ladder. This image reinforces the notion that God is
with the powerful. Theism teaches a kind of "trickle down" theology of grace.

Panentheism, on the other hand, teaches that God is in all
things and all things are in God. Thus God works *from the base,*
from the bottom up, from the inside out. *The Spirit comes from
within things.* This corresponds to group experiences in which

persons treat one another as equals in a circle, sharing a common story of pain and grace. Thus an Alcoholics Anonymous (AA) group operates on the understanding of where wisdom, and thereby divinity, can be found, as does a base community wherein peasant peoples share their insights about the Gospel, or a Dignity gathering where homosexual persons share with one another their stories of grace and liberation. Jesus models this kind of relationship with God when he preaches that the "reign of God" is already in our midst. His preaching to the poor was a recognition that God was truly "with them"—a celebration of panentheism over hierarchical theisms. (Emmanuel means "God-within-us.")

By emphasizing that the Spirit of God dwells in us all, creation spirituality liberates the mystic in us all. Panentheism is not only democratic, it is also ecological. Theism, on the other hand, reinforces anthropocentrism because it puts the human at the top of the ladder in an exclusive relationship with divinity. Panentheism celebrates the Divine Face, or the Cosmic Christ that is expressed in every creature. Panentheism renders our relationships with other species more mutual, reminding us that we are all beautiful, all interdependent, all necessary in a single web of life.

From Overly Institutional Religion to Living Mysticism

In the overdeveloped world, religion itself needs considerable liberation. Creation spirituality liberates religion from itself because it so awakens the mystic that the prophet must result from this awakening. A sharing of the fruits of one's contemplation, as the medievals used to say, results from true spirituality. The true creative spirit, the art-spirit of religion, comes alive through the practice of creation spirituality. With the return of play to religion all manner of empowerment and healing is possible. Dysfunctional behavior that so characterizes excessive institutionalization can be named for what it is. Denial ceases.

Creation spirituality liberates religion by reawakening the authentic communion of saints. By celebrating the deep wisdom

found in native peoples whose cosmology is invariably creation centered, creation spirituality liberates religion from its
racism and colonialism. The Four Paths of creation spirituality
provide a practical hermeneutic for interpreting our own rich
heritage and for making connections with other traditions'
rich mystical heritage. For example, our own Western Scriptures become revitalized. Themes of a Cosmic Christ theology
appear in the prologues to all four Gospels, the Easter narratives, Pentecost, the Book of Revelation, apocalyptic literature.
We experience all in a new and refreshingly substantive light.
(I have written about this in *The Coming of the Cosmic Christ*.) The
Beatitudes that Jesus preached in the Sermon on the Mount in
Matthew's Gospel might be seen anew in light of the Paths of
creation spirituality, as we discussed in chapter 4. Christ is re-
understood as Sophia (Wisdom), as we saw earlier.

In addition to liberating the way we read the Scriptures,
the perspective of creation spirituality can also liberate our
religious traditions, challenging them to greater authenticity.
Creation spirituality liberates Protestantism in general from
the excessive wordiness and headiness that identifies the "word
of God" exclusively with words in a book. Eckhart said—and
the radical reformers repeated this theme often—that "every
creature is a word of God and a book about God." It can also
deliver Protestantism from the deep strain of patriarchal mind-
set that runs through it and from an antimystical bias and an
a-cosmological way of seeing the world. This liberation can
assist Protestants in reclaiming the prophetic spirit that corresponds to the charisms of their founders.

Creation spirituality liberates Roman Catholicism from its
flirtations with fascism in this century, for it insists that not all
mysticisms are authentic, but only those that pass the test of
justice. It delivers Catholicism from its misogyny and its
unhealthy preoccupation with sexuality. By restoring sexuality
to a mystical and cosmological context that is more truly biblical, Catholicism can concentrate on the more important contributions it can make to planetary survival. Among these
would be a confirmation by praxis and theory of the validity of

a diversity of life-styles. Creation spirituality can help liberate from homophobia to a celebration of diversity. The creation spirituality critique can help Catholicism correct an excessively verbal liturgical practice, which has dominated since Vatican II, by placing worship into a more cosmological, bodily, and mystical setting. The return of mystery to Western worship would be a welcome way to revitalize imagination and compassionate practice.

Creation spirituality also challenges Roman Catholicism by asking whether by incorporating a more creation-spiritual perspective, it would not be more catholic in the true sense of the word—more universal and more respectful of diverse cultural expressions of Catholicism. In this way, this church tradition would correspond more to the Nicene Creed, which speaks of belief in a "Catholic" faith, not a Roman one.

From Sexism to Gender Justice

Religion often legitimizes the oppression of women with a kind of divine sanction. In contrast, creation spirituality celebrates women's wisdom and experience. Creation spirituality, for example, takes seriously those deeply cosmological and feminist texts of the Scriptures known as "Wisdom" literature, which come from North Africa where a Mother Goddess was worshiped before the Israelite people were formed. Listen to a few of those texts and see how they move the heart.

> From everlasting I was firmly set,
>   from the beginning, before earth came into being.
> The deep was not, when I was born,
>   there were no springs to gush with water.
> Before the mountains were settled,
>   before the hills, I came to birth. (Prov. 8:23–25)

> I came forth from the mouth of the Most High,
>   and I covered the earth like mist.
> I had my tent in the heights,
>   and my throne in a pillar of cloud.

Alone I encircled the vault of the sky,
　　and I walked on the bottom of the deeps.
Over the waves of the sea and over the whole earth,
　　And over every people and nation I have held
　　　　sway. . . .
Approach me, you who desire me,
　　and take your fill of my fruits. . . .
They who eat me will hunger for more,
　　and they who drink me will thirst for more.
　　　　　　　　　　　　　(Sir. 24:3–10, 19, 21)

Who can read these texts and remain unmoved? One reason they move us so profoundly is that they are so deeply cosmological.

Creation spirituality celebrates the fact that Jesus and certain unique men in history have also been "feminist" in the sense that they were attuned to the injustice inflicted on women simply because they were women. Women's experience in theory and practice is celebrated by creation spirituality. Because of the creation spirituality movement, the great works of the women mystics of the West have been made available in English translation for the first time. Consider, for example, the contributions of Hildegard of Bingen whose books on science, cosmology, holistic medicine, Scripture, and history, as well as her thirty-nine paintings and seventy-two songs and an opera— all created by her in the twelfth century—went almost unnoticed by male-dominated theological schools for eight centuries. Creation spirituality is sensitive to the sin of sexism, knowing that a redemption of our culture cannot occur without the contribution of that half of the human race that has suffered the most.

The pedagogy of creation spirituality is explicitly feminist, including process and experience and body along with ideas. Creation spirituality celebrates creativity and the motherhood of all persons. The sin of sexism is thus attacked at its root. Sexism is so insidious because it lurks in our innermost beings and imaginations and institutions.

Creation spirituality also recognizes the need of men for
liberation, including liberation from masculine stereotyping.
The more I experience male liberation groups, the more I
would say that men who are seeking authentic freedom are, in
fact, looking for ways to *recover the mystic again.* Sexist and patriarchal systems of education, the military, politics, economics,
and religion have robbed men in our culture of their right to
mystical experience. Creation spirituality can help men to reawaken their mystical consciousness, to let go of the wounded
boy that was once a mystic playing in the universe, and to allow
the grieving of the wounded male heart to take place, thus overcoming the lie that "big boys don't cry."

Creation spirituality also helps men to regain their mysticism by honoring the male mystics of the Western tradition
who were as much prophet as mystic—whether Jesus or Isaiah,
Eckhart or Aquinas, Dante or Francis, Martin Luther King, Jr.,
or Pablo Casals. Ultimately, women depend on themselves for
their own liberation, but from a cultural point of view, women
cannot be fully liberated without men also being freed from
their servitude to patriarchy. Part of male liberation consists
in dealing with homophobia, the irrational fear of the homosexual, which invariably stems from fear of the homosexual
dimension *within oneself.* Creation spirituality critiques the
sin of homophobia and, by celebrating the diversity within
creation, allows the homosexual to be homosexual. This frees
the heterosexual to be at home with his or her sexuality
without projection and prejudice toward those of a different
sexual orientation. Justice cannot stop at the door of sexual
discrimination.

From Unemployment to Good Work

Unemployment is one of the great evils in human life for it
prevents a person from returning her or his gift to the community. Work is about that: returning one's gift to the community.
The irony about all unemployment that I have witnessed,

whether in the urban areas of America, or on the streets of Rio de Janeiro, or in the countryside of Ireland, is this: there is always work that needs to be done for the well-being of a society, and there are always people who need good work. But the political will and imagination for bringing the two together is so often lacking. The unemployed increase in number everywhere—yet workers are needed everywhere. Where good work is lacking, self-doubt, self-hatred, crime, violence, alcohol and drug abuse abound. Why have our societies failed to move out of unemployment to full and good employment?

The ways in which we define work, and prepare people for work (education and training) have much to do with the squeezing out of some from work. Education as we define it in the West is generally suited only for work as defined in an industrial or postindustrial society. Not included in this understanding are *the healing arts*.* The healing arts are about ritual, art as meditation, community organizing, and community celebrations. These arts could assist any society in cutting its health care costs drastically; in putting people back to good work gardening, massaging, making music in neighborhoods, caring for the sick, assisting the handicapped in their own liberation, making lively the days of the aged ones (called "the treasured ones" by native peoples), caring for the very young, assisting single parents, helping the addicted to liberate themselves, teaching the illiterate to read and encouraging others to become educated, assisting young adults through rites of passage and in ways to respond to their call from the universe for work and relationship, and calling forth the healing of society's forgotten ones. Creation spirituality is all about the healing arts, and therefore, it is about putting people to good work again. Only a finite number of cars can or ought to be manufactured

---

*I recently met an aboriginal woman in Australia who said, "In our culture [which has lasted more than 50,000 years], people work four hours a day, and the rest of the day we make things." What things do they make? Primarily, art and ritual.

in this world, but when it comes to creativity—to healing and celebrating, to beauty and self-expression—the human species has an *infinite* number of possibilities.

From an Anthropocentric and Nondemocratic Capitalism to an Earth-Centered Economics

While "First World" countries find themselves currently gloating over the obvious failures of "Second World" nations to feed their peoples and to provide needed goods and services, the bills are still to come due for the failures of advanced capitalism as well. The ecological bills are rapidly descending on us as we begin the process of "denying the denial" that has dominated our economic system's attitude toward the destruction of the biosphere—a reality that is the result of the overdeveloped world's excessive emissions of carbon dioxide from automobiles and industry and its tearing down of forests and rain forests the world over. The poisoned air and water and soil cannot withstand continued laissez-faire capitalist attitudes. The *Exxon Valdez* is just one more warning about the danger the earth faces at the hands of excessively powerful and anthropocentric multinational corporations.

A nondemocratic capitalism—one that wraps itself in democratic sloganeering in its efforts to deceive the middle classes—is always hierarchical and adultist in its mentality. The young and the beginner—those without capital—are automatically squeezed out of such a system. For them, if they are lucky, there are crumbs from the top of the ladder and that is all. In such a system those who have get more and those who have not get even less. One young man in an urban ghetto was recently asked: "Why the gangs? Why the drugs?" His response was: "There is nothing else to do here. There is no other way up the ladder." The tragic demise of generation after generation of young African American and Native American men whether by drugs, crime, or prison is a poignant commentary on the failures of a less-than-democratic capitalism. A "war against drugs" heralded by our political leaders sounds ominously similar to other "wars" of the past twenty-five years such as the "war against poverty." Why the constant military imagery? Have we no imagination left for nonmilitary efforts? These "wars" cannot be won by military rhetoric or military spending. A society needs to open the hearts of its young people, giving them a reason for living and developing their gifts: gifts destined for the cosmos itself. Thus war is an inadequate category for the adventure we seek: the correct category is cosmology, which alone holds the power to give our young people a vision greater than consumerism offers.

Such a vision is that of an emerging earth community and its *need for the young to help save it.* The young today are, more than ever, the last great hope for the planet. We cannot waste them to a system that is so narrow that it defines economics (which means keeping a household) by facile numbers about stocks, bonds, capital, and money. The economics of the future must be defined by the wealth, which is the health, of Mother Earth and her children, especially the children yet to come. Creation spirituality calls us to such an economic vision. By insisting on the universal principle of letting go—that we are all capable of it and called to it, and that we can ritualize it for communities of small or large scale—creation spirituality provides us with a tool for resisting greed and converting it to justice making. By encouraging creativity in the service of justice making and celebration, creation spirituality offers us processes by which models of small business and creative commerce can serve and not pollute our spiritual and physical environments.

From the Fantasy Dream Life of Advertising to an Authentic Eschatology about Justice

Thomas Berry rightly talks of our culture as being one of a "fantasized dream life." This is the nature of a consumer culture where so much imagination, money, and creativity is put into the effort to create a dream life for people in order to get them to buy things. Whether it is the perfect sports car taking turns on totally empty highways (the people who film these commercials must get up awfully early in the morning to find such empty highways these days), or the perfectly built male standing almost naked in front of the mirror shaving with the all-perfect razor, or the ideally shaped woman eating her breakfast cereal with smiles and perfect, shiny teeth—it is all directed at our fantasy life. And it often reaches the target.

What is the result? I believe it is that true eschatology is driven out. *Eschatology* comes from the Greek word for the "future"—true eschatology is a *dream life about a better future.* But the better future that so appeals to our imaginations and dreams is not one of better goods but *of more justice.* The prophets dreamed of a world where "justice would flow like waters," and Hildegard of Bingen believed that "we shall awaken from our dullness and arise vigorously toward justice." That is the authentic dream life of a people—their dreams for a better community, a more whole and joyful community, a "beloved community," to use Martin Luther King, Jr.'s, image: a community without sexism, racism, colonialism, adultism, or anthropocentrism. A pseudo-dream life banishes such a dream. It fills our fantasies with a different agenda, one that preoccupies our imaginations and distracts us from more noble dreams.

Creation spirituality, on the other hand, seeks to restore eschatology in its fullest sense—it fuels a vision of a New Creation, of a transformed society with transformed education and worship and work and relationships. Like any eschatological vision, it also encounters considerable opposition and distortion of its message by those who are more invested in the old dream than in a dream of full participation.

One wonders whether this list of "liberations *from*" does not name the spiritual impoverishment that lies behind the political/cultural impotency of the overdeveloped world; whether these issues do not constitute the causes behind the continued exploitation of the so-called "Third World" by the "First World" peoples. The corresponding "liberations *to*" offers an agenda of hope and empowerment that might reverse the servitude to which the overdeveloped world is subject. Just as the slave master is a victim of slavery, albeit a less obvious one, so the overdeveloped world is a victim of its own worldview.

❖ 8 ❖

Toward a Spirituality of the Americas

One lesson I have learned in writing this essay is *how much* creation spirituality and liberation theology have in common, that is, how *American* both movements are. In using "American," I do not mean "United States" at the expense of Canada or Latin American nations. I mean "American" in the sense of two continents bound together—the only two continents like this—spanning North and South, like a full human body, head and trunk. The Americas have unique gifts for the world at this time in history. They have unique gifts for the Christian Church, emerging from a fall/redemption spiritual slumber of several hundred years.

The Americas include prime examples of so-called "First World" and "Third World" nations. What a pity that so much money, military might, and political rhetoric has been wasted between these continents on the issue of perceived "Second World" intervention instead of on the issue of *how the land of the Americas could become a model for "First World"–"Third World" cooperation, letting go, and realignment.* What an opportunity this land offers for moving from hegemony of the overdeveloped nations over underdeveloped nations to justice *between* nations.

North and South America share a common life-and-death struggle. This struggle is not only the obvious one in the streets of El Salvador and among the campesinos of Brazil—it is also a struggle in the corridors of "First World" multinational hamburger restaurants, in the boardrooms of banks, on the floors of stockmarkets, and in the stockholder meetings of corporations in Germany, Holland, England, Japan, and the United

States. It is a struggle in the hearts and bodies of North Americans who are becoming addicted to drugs from Latin America or succumbing to despair and poverty.

The Americas: a Common History of Struggle

The peril of our times calls for letting go and reconciliation. If the president of the USSR can call for *perestroika,* if the United States and the USSR can become friendly again, why can the same spirit not prevail between the United States and Latin America? After all, we Americans share a common landmass and a common history of struggle against European colonialism. And why can the spirituality of the Americas not create together a new expression of church? After all, we share many common spiritual roots and struggles:

1. The Americas share an experience of European colonialism. The people native to the land of the Americas were victims of a genocide seldom if ever matched on this planet. Their numbers were reduced from 80 million when Columbus landed to 10 million fifty years later. Today, this genocide continues in Guatemala and elsewhere and is felt on North American reservations, in the sad price of alcoholism, drug addiction, in youth despair and suicide, and in the Vatican's unmentionably insensitive efforts to canonize Junipero Serra, a Franciscan missionary who colonized Indians, beat them (even after the governor had forbidden beatings of Indians) and contributed heavily to the destruction of their culture in California. Despite this holocaust and continuous oppression, the wisdom of these people has never died out. Today there is a resurgence of religious practice among native peoples and a new appreciation by white scholars of the immense cultural achievements of these highly developed civilizations, including their agricultural, economic, political, and artistic accomplishments. When Dominican missionary Bartholomew de las Casas proclaimed in the sixteenth century that the Indian civilization was far superior to that of Spain, he was speaking a

literal truth that has yet to be understood in Europe or in America. This is where a true *ecclesiogenesis,* to use a term coined by liberation theology, can occur: a rebirth of church that *incorporates* rather than destroys the wisdom of the people of the Americas.

Historically, both North and South America underwent the traumas of colonialism. The North Americans conquered colonialism earlier than the Latin Americans did and, unfortunately, have reversed roles. How ironic it is that the United States, so proud of its revolution of 1776 against British colonialism, turned around in the nineteenth and twentieth centuries to become the imperial power dictating to Latin American nations. The United States colonized Latin America, often with the kind of cruelty that a wounded child effects on others when that child becomes a "killer adult." What would happen if the Americas could break the habit of colonialism and of empire building? In the nineties we are observing the Soviet Empire breaking up—is it not time for the United States empire that dominates Latin America to do the same? In April 1988, over 100 Christian pastors, lay leaders, and theologians from around Central America issued a document called the "Kairos Document." In it they image the struggle of the poor against the "idols of the empire":

> In the process of maturing in their historical con-
> sciousness with the help of their faith, Central
> America's poor came to find out that the God of
> Western Christian society was not the God of Jesus,
> but rather an idol of the Empire.... The Central
> American poor at this time are serving as witnesses
> and martyrs for the God of Jesus, the God of the
> poor.... They are a living prophecy...that invites
> the Christian churches to abandon the Empire's gods
> and become converted to the true God.

Can the "First World" let go of its empire and thus free itself as well as those colonized by it?

2. It is obvious that North and South America share a common geography that is growing more intimate daily as the world shrinks. This is happening not only because of rapid travel and communication, but also because of the interdependence between the suffering rain forests of Brazil and the air pollution of Mexico City or New York City. Consider the following facts: since 1950, half the world's tropical forests have disappeared—37 percent in Latin America; 66 percent in Central America; 38 percent in Asia; 52 percent in Africa. This devastation brings with it increased erosion of the soil, drying of the climate, destruction of agriculture. The main cause of this disappearance has been policies of "First World" countries. The carbon dioxide occasioned by North American lifestyles, as well as the destruction of the rain forest by northern corporations, is further evidence of the shadow side of interconnectivity. All of us are enmeshed in the ecological crisis. The shameful efforts to secretly dump waste materials—including nuclear waste—from overdeveloped countries into underdeveloped ones is another example of the interconnectivity we share by common geography.

3. Both North and South America find their youth in crisis. In the South there are estimated to be millions of youth living alone on the streets of Brazil. In the North we find an epidemic of despair, violence, and suicide among our teenagers. The rates of drug and alcohol addictions and teen pregnancies are soaring. Youths are filling our prisons to overflowing. Would not a healthy spirituality wrestle head-on with ways to heal and empower our youth, awakening hope and self-discipline? Would not a healthy spirituality seek to develop new forms of worship that offer opportunity to the young? Would not a healthy spirituality find effective ways to redirect money spent on militarism to monies for job making and job training, to reinvent work for the unemployed masses of young people, to reinvent education so that it serves the *whole* person, and to create good work as well?

If adults lack the fire inside to bring about these changes, then perhaps the time has arrived for the youth of the world who find themselves excluded from an adultist scheme of politics and economics, of education and religion, to opt out of the adultist culture altogether and to start their own subculture. One that will not be based on the same economic presuppositions. One in which they grow their own food, make their own clothes, birth their own education and entertainment, and celebrate their own rituals.

4. North and South America share the drug crisis. Latin America would not be so compelled to produce this lucrative cash crop if North Americans did not provide so rich a market. North Americans need spiritual resources to overcome their need for this addiction and Latin Americans need alternative cash crops. Would an awakened spirituality not assist this common need of letting go?

5. North and South America are linked by a common economic debt. Latin America is said to owe North American banks about $300 billion, which is, after all, less than the United States spends annually on weapons and armies. We are told that if U.S. banks were to let go of this debt our banking system would collapse. Maybe it is time for a banking breakthrough, for a new system of banking that is more global, more inclusive of the non-rich nations, more just, and more realistic. Certainly no banker realistically expects Latin America to ever repay this debt. Two years ago Latin Americans paid $70 billion in interest alone with no payment on the principal. Is this debt not a continuation of the servitude that Europe has imposed on the Americas since their colonization? Why not a breakthrough that will "get the monkey off" Latin American economies, and thus free them to enter the world economy not as debtors but as partners? Haven't these nations struggled long enough in their slavery toward foreign usurers? Has there ever been a more propitious time to declare what the Bible calls a "Jubilee Year" in which all debts are erased and relationships among equals can begin anew?

I recall visiting the large and ancient basilica of St. John Lateran in Rome this past year. It was a Sunday morning and the worshipers were all huddled at the front of the huge church; they numbered about 175. Wandering through the vast marble expanses of the church were tourists from all over the world. I listened to one of the tour guides tell a group: "Look up at the ceiling. The gold was brought from Peru." Later I visited the large church of St. Mary Major. There too the gold on the ceilings was brought from the Americas. I find this story to be quite archetypal. If the Roman Catholic Church were serious about economic justice in the "Third World" it might choose to return some of the gold confiscated from the Americas over the centuries. Such a symbolic gesture might pave the way for the conversion that the banking systems of overdeveloped nations must undergo.

The Americas in Search of an Alternative Education Model

European models of education from Kant and Descartes are not adequate for the imaginative modes of learning by which the aboriginal peoples and African American peoples learn and by which many of the young need to learn: that is, by stories and by participation. The Native American way of learning is less dualistic than the ways we have borrowed from Europe.

Philosophy in the Americas is not heady—though it is not anti-intellectual either. It is often called "pragmatic," which is to say, anti-idealist and anti-patriarchal. There is a necessary *mother component* to American philosophy and this may well be due to the spirit of the primal peoples of this land whose religion has been called by Frederick Turner, "aboriginal mother love." Process is required in all learning situations. The emphasis on *praxis* in liberation theology and in creation spirituality is an expression of the pragmatism of our peoples, for spirituality *is experience,* which is meant to precede theory and to test it.

Creativity is important to any philosophy in the Americas. One can feel the pulse of creativity in a young nation like

Canada, for example, and in many cities in the United States. The artist beholds first and judges later. The artist learns by trial and error. The artist honors discipline but shies away from asceticism. It is understood among all native tribes that every member is a creative person and that all human work involves co-creating with the universe. Paulo Friere comments on the importance of creativity to the oppressed when he says:

> The people must be challenged to discover their historical existence through the critical analysis of their cultural production, their art and their music. Once they perceive that their music is as much culture and art as the music of Beethoven, they can break out of the dimension of inferiority that prevents them from participating in the true creation of their society.

In the North, women have been working at conquering their inferiority feelings toward their artistic accomplishments and celebrating their "historical existence" by rediscovering their art. Judy Chicago's work is just one example. Where would the African Americans be without their cultural achievements of music, humor, and art?

Liberation theology brings about the awakening of persons and communities through a process of education so different from our inherited educational projects that it boasts a new name, *conscientization,* the awakening of consciousness that occurs when we break through our old and often inherited concepts of who we are and what our responsibilities are. When adults learn to read by means of issues such as the "peasant's house" in contrast to the "landowner's house," reading takes on immediate political and imaginative impact. The strength of the insights gained drive out any masochistic tendencies inherited from a sadistic society.

Creation spirituality also offers an alternative education model. It consciously lets go of the paradigm of seeing the world in patriarchal and dualistic terms. This empowers because it puts us, our problems, and our gifts, in the context of the cosmic story and because it affirms our basic beauty and capacity to return blessing for blessing. It teaches us of our rights and our responsibilities in being here.

In practice creation spirituality heals the anthropocentric educational model that dominates "First World" education and creates abstracted persons who can so easily ignore their feelings and those of others. In other words, creation spirituality teaches compassion. It does so by placing the human agenda at both the personal and historical-communal level in the context of a living cosmology. When this volatile mix is added to art as meditation, the mystic-prophet in the learner is awakened and released. Cosmology means that science, mysticism, and art come together to awaken us about our common origins and therefore common goals. This education truly awakens over-developed people to awe and wonder, to empowerment and social responsibility.

To work with scientists and artists, with ritual makers and native peoples, with feminists and social activists constitutes what Boff terms a "different way of doing theology" and in fact constitutes becoming a different kind of theologian. Says Boff: "Rather than introducing a new theological method, liberation theology is a new way of being a theologian. . . . Theology (not the theologian) comes afterward; liberating practice comes first." Creation spirituality affects the theologian himself or herself—it reconstitutes them in the matrix of the culture as a whole and does not allow the theologian to settle as a citizen merely of a "religious" culture. Both creation spirituality and liberation theology find education to be the heart of liberation and both movements insist on critiquing the dominant models of education. Education itself can and needs to be liberated.

The Americas: A Shared Wilderness Mysticism

North and South Americans share a creation mysticism in common. Why has Ernesto Cardenal, the Nicaraguan poet and prophet, entitled his recently completed *chef d'oevre, Cantico*

Cosmico? Why was the term Cosmic Christ used for the very first time in 1906 in the United States? (Though the concept of the Cosmic Christ was ancient, the actual term came out of American theology.) Why has the creation-centered tradition of spirituality been resuscitated in the United States? Why has this land birthed pantheistic poets of the caliber of Walt Whitman, Emily Dickenson, Robinson Jeffers, William Everson, Robert Frost, Adrienne Rich, Audre Lorde, Denise Levertov, and Wendell Berry, and such writers like David Thoreau, John Muir, Rachel Carson, Annie Dillard, Barry Lopez, Alice Walker, and Thomas Berry? This is a land where the cosmos and divine have never been successfully sundered as they were in Europe. Dualism is, in fact, foreign to our spirituality. Is there any dualism to be found among Latin American novelists such as Jorge Arnado and Isabel Allende, or among musicians such as Victor Jara, Carlos Mejia Godoy, or Violeta Parra, or among poets such as Pablo Neruda, Julia Esquivel, Pedro Casadaliga, or Rigoberto Lopez Perez?

Barry Lopez, in a brilliant essay on "The Passing Wisdom of Birds," describes how Cortez and his men, while laying waste to the ancient and most beautiful city in the world, the "Aztec Byzantium—Tenochtitlan," or Mexico City, also destroyed the millions of birds in the city. He comments on what it is we lose when nature is debased:

> We stand to lose the focus of our ideals. We stand to lose our sense of dignity, of compassion, even our sense of what we call God. The philosophy of nature we set aside eight thousand years ago in the Fertile Crescent we can, I think, locate again and greatly refine in North America. The New World is a landscape still overwhelming in the vigor of its animals and plants, resonant with mystery. It encourages, still, an enlightened response toward indigenous cultures that differ from our own, whether Aztecan, Lakotan, lupine, avian, or invertebrate. By broadening our

sense of the intrinsic worth of life and by cultivating respect for other ways of moving toward perfection, we may find the sense of resolution we have been looking for, I think, for centuries.

What Lopez says of North America applies to all the Americas. And indeed to most Asian, African and South Pacific lands and their peoples. He says that our land invites us from anthropocentrism to cosmology.

Americans know that the wilderness is something sacred. And that we humans hold a wilderness inside—if only we would honor it. One is reminded of the prophet Hosea who declared that "I [Yahweh] will call you out to the wilderness and there speak to you heart to heart." Or of the Song of Songs wherein the lovers emerge hand in hand "from the wilderness" of human loving, which is also divine love. The American passion for the wilderness awakens a sense of Dionysian consciousness which in turn challenges European definitions of spirituality. Ecstasy frightens the Apollonian mentality, but it is, as I make clear in *Whee! We, wee All the Way Home,* as good a name as any for God experience. Poet William Everson offers an evaluation of the Dionysian poet's fate in our culture that parallels, I believe, what one might come to expect while bringing a Dionysian theology to spirituality:

> The Dionysian poet always suffers at the hands of the Apollonian critics of his own time. He brings this material from the unconscious, and to them he violates their principles, and they find this wretched. And they fear this material because they feel that, as the masters of the cultural continuum, they have to protect its purity against these outrages. . . . Henry James when he first read the *Leaves of Grass*, set down as the opening words of his review: "This will never do!"
>
> I point to Isaiah, the supreme religious Dionysian poet. And then you have Dante, who is the supreme Christian Apollonian poet. For me, I prefer an Isaiah to a Dante because I feel he is closer to God.

Creation spirituality's gift and burden lies in its being both more Dionysian and more prophetic than the dominant theological paradigm from Europe.

The Americas and the Birthing of a Church

North and South America are partners in what Penny Lernoux has called in her very important book, *The People of God: The Struggle for World Catholicism.* The largest Roman Catholic church exists in Brazil and the wealthiest, best educated, and most active Roman Catholics live in the United States. Is there not a natural affinity between these two bodies? World Catholicism might more closely approximate gospel values in the future if the morality of the "preferential option for the poor" preached by the Latin American Church were *practiced* in a renewed North American church. Ecumenism is far more advanced in the Americas than it is in Europe, where old memories and nonpracticing Christians abound.

Atheism, I am convinced, is a European invention. It exists in the head, where so many European philosophers have lived and have told the rest of us to live. I have never met a native person who was an atheist; they are too close to creation to have gone untouched by its numinosity. Only an anthropocentric civilization could have invented something called atheism. Ninety-nine percent of atheism, I am convinced, is antitheism and anticlericalism (the two, theism and clericalism, go together nicely, since both rely on Jacob's Ladder mentalities to survive). Much practical atheism is a rank denial of human rights as we see in the military in El Salvador today; or it is a religion of empire building, such as that often carried on in the name of fundamentalist Christianity. Panentheism is the alternative to theism, atheism, and antitheism, and the peoples of the Americas know panentheism well.

Ecclesiogenesis means the birthing of a church, of a people becoming church in a new way. The spirit births the church in ever-new ways, for as Leonardo Boff writes, "The history of the church is genuine history: the creation of never-before-

experienced novelty. . . . Our situation will have to be understood in the light of the Holy Spirit." It should be remembered,
of course, that the Spirit births the church—it is not the church
that births the Spirit. Recently a young man told me that he was
struggling deeply over whether to stay in the church or leave it.
I suggested to him that there was a third option—that of birthing a church. Ecclesiogenesis will challenge many to creativity,
especially the young. A church renewed by a spiritual vision is
just one area in which a renaissance needs to occur in our time.

Hildegard of Bingen says that we are co-creators with God
in everything we do. Putting our awakened and liberated gifts
to the service of renewing the church is an important vocation
in our time, an important act of the Via Transformativa. If we
cannot transform our institutions—of which church is a significant one—we are lost and most likely the earth itself is also
doomed. Creation spirituality contributes its share to ecclesiogenesis at many levels. One is at the level of worship. Since I
have written in *The Coming of the Cosmic Christ* at some length
about what is needed to renew worship in the West, I will not
repeat myself here. In that book, I outline six principles for
authentic worship. Creation spirituality, because it honors the
ancient rituals of native peoples and listens to their wisdom,
because it teaches participants to rediscover the empowerment
that comes from ritual, and because it places ritual in a cosmological context, has much to offer in helping religion move
beyond verbosity to living ritual.

While ecumenism among Christian churches often seems
at a standstill, I believe that something very deep is happening
at the grassroots. The heart of it is what I call the "ecumenism
of comedy," as distinct from the "ecumenism of tragedy." In all
church bodies today there is a deep split between justice-
oriented people and fundamentalists. The latter get more
vocal, even though they constitute a tiny minority in these traditions, and more energy gets wasted trying to mollify them.
What will need to happen is for divisions in the church
denominations to take place in order to allow new connectings
to occur, linking those from various traditions who agree that

justice is a constitutive element of the gospel. Joseph Meeker describes how when communities are split up, there are often two responses. The first is tragedy, which often ends in funerals, as in *Romeo and Juliet*. The second response is comedy, often characterized by weddings, as in Dante's *Divine Comedy*. I anticipate a score of church weddings in the nineties, an "ecumenism of comedy" that begins in the hearts and minds of church people at the grassroots.

Creation spirituality also assists the renewal of the church by restoring feminist wisdom and practice and the stories of our women mystic-prophets, to a place of honor in our tradition. The model of education that creation spirituality has developed would be a marvelous way of creating a truly alternative model of Christian education—one that offered hope to the young and the planet by refusing to merely imitate the prevailing secular model of education. This model includes the numinous and the experience of the sacred that is inherent to any cosmological tradition of learning. Such a tradition recovers the child, the divine mystic within all students, and measures educational success by the effectiveness of our efforts at justice making and compassion. It is a feminist model of education—one that honors process and feeling along with critical analysis and conceptualization, all put at the service of transformation.

Moreover, this model of education can rightly be called a "Wisdom School," since it inculcates us in more than knowledge (which our species is saturated with); it teaches wisdom, rules for living in the universe, ways to open and strengthen the heart and to create harmony with earth, self, other species, and other humans, and with the creative "mind" of the universe. There is a desperate need for such "Wisdom Schools" at all levels of society and education.

At the foundation of the movement of *ecclesiogenesis* in liberation theology is the *base community* movement. These communities represent what Boff calls "a new experience of church, of community, of communion of persons within the more legitimate (in the strict sense of the word) ancient tradition." The small group builds community more effectively than institutional parochial structures can. These communities form a polar tension to institutional structures but are not meant to rival them as such. Yet they "constitute the true and authentic presence of the Catholic Church." Even if much of Latin American Catholicism is characterized by the absence of ordained ministers and formal Eucharist, the people of God give birth to a new expression of church. The term *base* means that "the church is not being thought of from the top down, but from the bottom up, from the grassroots." Within this base community numerous ministries are taken up in the name of Christ and the church such as community leadership and coordination, catechesis, organizing liturgy, caring for the sick, teaching people to read and write, looking after the poor. Decision making is not done from the top down but from consensus among the people "in a circular, participatory model."

In creation spirituality we distinguish between two models of spirituality and social organization: "Climbing Jacob's Ladder" or "Dancing Sara's Circle." The latter model is participatory, circular, close to the earth, egalitarian and self-healing, self-motivating and self-organizing, like the universe itself. The Climbing Jacob's Ladder model is intrinsically elitist, hierarchical, and competitive, since only a few can make it to the top of the ladder. It is also antiearth; God is exclusively a "Sky God" being a remnant of patriarchal and sexist theological thinking. In practice, the Dancing Sara's Circle model corresponds to the base community model in liberation theology. The Sara's Circle model corresponds to the scientific theory of the Self-Organizing Universe, whereas the Jacob's Ladder model better fits the Newtonian and pre-Newtonian views of the world as a series of flat planes (no one puts a ladder on a curved surface). A contemporary cosmology definitely favors a Sara's Circle organizational model.

In addition, creation spirituality works out of the base to the extent that it awakens those at the bottom—the *anawim*—to their own leadership potential; worship and teaching do not come "from above" but arise from the experience of people. By encouraging the mystic in every person and by offering praxis for eliciting this mystic, creation spirituality promotes empowerment at the base. Creation spirituality insists that *all are mystics* and *all are prophets* and thus all persons are called both to their own dignity *and* to responsibility and leadership. How this leadership takes place will be different in a "First World" and predominantly middle-class culture than in a "Third World" culture, which is so often divided sharply between rich and poor. For example, academic degrees play a greater role in overdeveloped countries for they allow persons "from the base"—women, racial/ethnic minorities, and, in the church, lay persons—to enter the institutions of religion, education, medicine, law, politics, and media with greater credibility. Adult education seminars and workshops offer the opportunity for awakening busy persons who may already be in positions of influence whether clergy or teachers or artists or lawyers or doctors or community leaders, thereby granting them a new vision by which to renew their work worlds. By such workshops professionals can let go of one paradigm and embark upon another. As Eckhart put it: "A person works in a stable: that person has a breakthrough; what does she do? She returns to the stable."

In the "First World" true education for change is more a matter of *infiltration* than it is in the "Third World" where far fewer options exist for sociological influence. Some creation spirituality people reenter an active parish life while others opt to create alternative educational or worship groups, encouraging ritual to emerge from the spiritually disenfranchised. Base communities are less visible in the "First World" than in the "Third World." This is not necessarily a bad thing but just a different situation. In overdeveloped cultures this work for an alternative paradigm often needs to be subtle, a quiet leaven within societies' structures of media and education, of science and economics, of politics and religion, of health care and psychology.

The base community movements are a reminder to all peoples that life is not life without community and that community is built on the struggle to put shared values into practice and not on the compulsion to shop or to make money together. The Spirit works through the community and very often through the "least" in the community. Sara's Circle, not Jacob's Ladder, predominates. We all need to stay close to the earth, close to our common roots, to remain vital and full of spirit. If we do not, if we succumb to ladder climbing and success addictions, the Spirit cannot work through us.

The base community is the cell organization of the organism known as "the popular church" in Latin America. It is more basic than are geographic parishes, which do not respond to the people's stories and struggle and passion and do not empower people as does the base community experience. In the base communities, the experience of community is more important than the emphasis on societal conformity found in most parish contexts. Leonardo Boff asks the question: "May one arouse and nourish the expectation that the whole church may one day be transformed into a community?" and he comments that the new phenomenon that base communities represent "is still just beginning, still in process. It is not accomplished reality. Pastors and theologians, take warning! Respect the new way that is appearing on the horizon. Do not seek at once to box this phenomenon within theological-pastoral categories distilled from other contexts and other ecclesial experiences. Instead, assume the attitude of those who would see, understand, and learn."

Historically, a great impulse to the base community in Latin America has been the shortage of trained professionals in ministry (that is, priests and sisters). This shortage is increasing as the populations of the "Third World" expand and as fewer persons are entering the all-male, all-celibate Catholic priesthood around the world. But what has occurred in the base communities with their emphasis on leadership *at the base* is that the Spirit remakes the entire church—including our very images and theologies of ministry and priesthood—in a new wave of spiritual leadership.

Base Communities in the Overdeveloped Nations

A question for "First World" peoples is the following: Are we also experiencing the emergence of our own kinds of base communities? Are they also happening as a historical and sociological phenomenon rising from the needs of the people? I believe that this is the case, that the Spirit is truly moving in overdeveloped countries and that the Spirit operates here most visibly *out of the wounds of oppression.*

I gave a series of lectures and workshops in San Diego on the theme "Creation Spirituality: A Movement of Hope in a Time of Despair." Organized by various movements and groups including the Society of Friends, the University of San Diego, United Campus Christian Ministries, and others, the numerous events were well attended. After the last lecture, a white-bearded man stood up and said: "I have lived in San Diego for over fifty years and this week marks the first time we have ever brought together all the movements for social renewal in this city—ecological, feminist, peace movements, gay and lesbian, church movements, Jungians, and so on." I was struck by this statement and what it taught me about how a creation spirituality movement can serve to unite other movements of liberation. Creation spirituality provides common ground and common language within which many other communities of liberation can join hands and forces, souls and bodies, to release the spirit and develop the vision we need to bring about effective liberation and transformation. Because it is ecumenical and yet names the mystical journey that is all of ours, because it is not elitist but is found in ordinary person's deepest experiences of joy and sorrow, creativity and compassion, creation spirituality can be utilized as an umbrella kind of movement to get artists and scientists, psychologists and street people, justice and ecological activists, native and black and white peoples, artists and mystics, together to form a larger constituency. Spirituality can ground us all.

Here are some examples of emerging base community groups in the "First World." They are not all explicitly Christian but they are all evidently spiritual. Many presume a practice of deep ecumenism or lead persons into such a practice.

Hospice

Hospice is a movement that deserves to be called a base community for it brings diverse persons together around a common task of dealing with death. It grants dying persons a human setting in which to bring their lives to a dignified end. Hospice necessarily deals with spiritual issues of fear and denial, of healing and reconciliation, of joy and letting go. Creativity and art-as-meditation is an important part of the work of hospice. Hospice denies the denial of death that is prevalent in overdeveloped countries where consumerism and materialism so often render life and its mysteries superficial. Hospice creates an authentic community experience where young and old, healthy and unhealthy, poor and comfortable, black and white come together in a context that is greater than any one person's agenda. People relinquish their Jacob's Ladder status to join the Sara's Circle that death urges on all of us.

AA Groups

AA groups and the groups they have spawned, such as Adult Children of Alcoholics, Overeaters Anonymous, Fundamentalist Anonymous, and so on perform a healing service using a Sara's Circle model. Their common ground is the storytelling that ensues. They bring about group and individual empowerment based on the common grief and suffering that addictions inflict on the addicted, their families, and friends. They are service oriented in the sense that their members serve one another as listeners when the crisis of addiction occurs. Empowerment arises from the wounds that exist within the group.

AA can be criticized for its excessively patriarchal religious imagery and language and its almost exclusive emphasis on the "word" as distinct from other kinds of healing rituals that could be employed, as well as for its almost nonexistent political, sexual, and class consciousness. All these weaknesses simply underscore the historical and cultural limits of its founders. Nevertheless, the movement has helped millions of persons. Those who appreciate the community created by this movement can love it enough to criticize it and bring about its renewal through some of the contributions that creation spirituality can offer.

Support Groups

Support Groups borrow from the successful Sara's Circle model of peer-group healing that AA has launched. These groups play a significant base community service in peoples' lives, ranging as they do from artist support groups to Vietnam Veterans' groups, from battered women's groups to Incest Survivors, as well as other groups for women and the growing male liberation movements. I believe these groups can all profit from learning some of the perspective and methods of creation spirituality.

Womenchurch

Womenchurch is truly an emerging base community for all those persons who seek "primary communities that nurture" and that go beyond the institutional church practice that is all too often "an occasion for sin rather than redemption" and whose forms of worship alienate by reason of their sexism and hierarchism, as Rosemary Ruether puts it. Womenchurch does not seek to be a separate sect or a schismatic movement, but to reclaim aspects of a biblical spirituality while going "behind it and beyond it" and providing a significant journey for liberating women and men alike from patriarchal religion. This vision would hopefully carry the people "beyond the hopes of modern male liberalism and socialism." Like creation spirituality, Womenchurch does not depend exclusively on the bible as a starting point, as liberation theology tends to do. This movement is ecumenical, including women of Protestant, Roman Catholic, and Jewish backgrounds.

Dignity

Dignity is the base community movement of gay and lesbian Catholics that has remained in the church, despite continued attack from the Vatican. The members of Dignity celebrate liturgy sometimes with and sometimes without an ordained priest (it is often a risky thing for ordained priests to participate in Dignity events). Members of Dignity offer support to one another by sharing their stories and other experiences of community. Of particular concern to Dignity is the hypocrisy they sense among churchmen who are themselves homosexual but who make orders or carry out orders that feed the demons of homophobia. Educating the public to its homophobia is an important part of the work of Dignity, but the most important education that takes place is that of eliminating internalized oppression. When homosexual persons internalize the value system of homophobia they become their own worst enemies. Thus, Dignity lives out the biblical injunction to "love your enemies"—in this case, oneself. Healthy communities of Dignity members reach out to other oppressed groups with a deeper sense of real compassion. In this way Dignity avoids becoming a kind of sect.

Reevaluation Counseling

Reevaluation Counseling is a very impressive worldwide movement that deals with the psychic pains of oppression of all kinds—the wounds of blue-collar persons, of Jews, of Catholics, of African Americans, of native peoples, of women, of war veterans, and so on. This movement is truly a base community for the sharing of stories and the application of a critical philosophy that raises consciousness about internalized oppression. The journeys to healing and wholeness that individuals undergo are invariably real and deep. True compassion—the ability to understand and wrestle with other people's suffering as well as our own—is the genuine result of their meetings, writings, and mutual support. Unlike many more "psychologically oriented" movements of healing, this movement boasts an explicit cosmology along with a highly developed sense of social consciousness.

Call to Action and the 8th of May Movement

In 1976 the National Conference of Catholic Bishops sponsored a kind of national pastoral council for the American Catholic Church entitled "Call to Action." In the spirit of American democracy, many grassroots persons spoke their minds on issues confronting church and society, but the progressive tone of the group embarrassed the bishops who let the process die. It did not go away, however, and has been carried on independently by a group active in Chicago. This group is now several thousand strong and is pushing for reforms within the church and is making connections with other renewal efforts emerging from base communities.

In some ways the Call to Action resurgence in the American church is like the 8th of May Movement (EMM) in Holland, and the two movements may well be merging. The Dutch movement, which calls itself "The Other Face of the Church," derives its name from the date on which John Paul II visited Holland in 1985. At that time the bishops of Holland declared that only "loyal Catholics" would be allowed to address the pope. Professor Catherina Halkes, the country's best-known feminist theologian, was refused permission to speak on behalf of Catholic women's organizations. In response, the EMM was launched. More than ten thousand persons attended the first meeting, and more than one hundred organizations, movements, and groups participate in the EMM. Their spoken objective is "to give face in the Netherlands to the church of Jesus Christ, as it shows itself in movements and groups that are looking for a new understanding of his liberating Gospel, that want to be guided by it and that want to dedicate themselves to a world of justice and peace." This group has aligned itself with issues of women's rights, of homosexual priests and theologians calling for a new understanding of sexuality and intimacy for all church members, of ecological movements, of study groups dealing with issues of cosmology and liberation. Many members of this movement work with persons with AIDS, with the homeless, the hungry, and with prostitutes.

Re-Creation of Base Community Movements in Latin America

There are efforts to re-create base community movements in Latin America within parish structures in North America, especially in parishes with large Hispanic populations, such as the parish of St. Pius in Chicago. Perhaps it is too early to evaluate the full import of this experiment, but it appears to be a sound effort to renew life among Catholics in the United States who are not middle class and yearn for an experience of community that goes beyond societal conformity. As the pool of male celibate ministers dries up, churches are being abandoned. The ironic result is that new forms of spiritual leadership are emerging—sisters, lay men and women, and married priests. In many ways these communities can be understood as base communities.

Friends of Creation Spirituality

Friends of Creation Spirituality, at the time of this writing, has more than one hundred identifiable "regional connectors" operating from *base groups* located in Australia, New Zealand, Canada, Ireland, England, and the United States. These groups sponsor rituals and workshops and provide a context within which stories are shared, community is fostered, and consciousness is raised around the themes and ideas of creation spirituality. Jim Conlon, program director at the Institute in Culture and Creation Spirituality, calls this movement an "informal non-organization," borrowing language from Saul Alinsky. The numbers of these "self-organizing" groups are increasing rapidly as more persons become on the one hand alienated by a lack of spiritual vision in society and church, and on the other, excited by the vision of creation spirituality, its ways of *praxis* and its potential for providing vision for other movements of social renewal: ecological, sexual, cosmological, youth, racial, and ethnic. None of these groups has developed in a "trickle-down fashion." All have emerged from the grass roots, at the base where people live, struggle, and worship.

Anglican and Protestant Parishes

Other institutions in the overdeveloped world with immense potential are Anglican and Protestant parishes. For example, consider that, historically, the black church kept the black community together, informing and renewing itself in the presence of oppression and racism all around it. In many places—alas!—the black church is no longer able to fulfill its prophetic function because the attention of young black men, owing to unemployment and despair, is so often given to gangs and the "fast money" offered by drug trading. But when the black church is alive and well—as it is in certain parts of all cities, for example—then it too is a base community that works to liberate the people.

I foresee that Protestant and Anglican parishes hold genuine potential as places for the development of base communities in creation spirituality. Why? Because they are often of a more intimate *size* than Roman Catholic parishes built around the few remaining celibate male priests. Given smallness, peoples' stories can be told and heard. Community and solidarity ensues. With women in the pulpits and leading rituals, there returns a genuine interest in, and demand for cosmology and mysticism and effective rituals. Many Protestants have been bereft of their own mystical roots for a long while and are demanding a return to those roots. The result is an awakening to a spirituality that corresponds to the protesting, prophetic charism of their tradition.

Protestant churches tend to be voluntary communities to a greater extent than many geographically based Catholic parishes. Those who desire creation spirituality can go out and find it. Just as Catholicism is engaging in some rather public

infighting between Vatican and liberation or creation spirituality theologians, so Protestants may expect some turmoil at the
local level where much of their ecclesial struggle is often
worked out. That is not necessarily a bad thing—a base community may be smaller than a parish, but if it coalesces around
shared values, ritual, and the *praxis* of justice making, it will be
very strong. One thinks of the amazing accomplishments of the
Church of the Saviour in Washington, of the Wellington
church in Chicago, or of the Community Christian Church in
Tiburon, California. The pastor of the Wellington church
writes: "Institutional churches as we know them are not an adequate religious center for people facing crises." I believe we can
expect a great gust of spiritual renewal of a mystical—prophetic kind from Protestant and Anglican churches renewed as
creation spirituality base communities.

Catholic Worker Houses

Another example of base communities in the "First World" are
Catholic Worker Houses. These communities, founded by
Dorothy Day in the mid-1930s, are under lay leadership and
consist of people who have chosen to live and work with the
poor. They are places of hospitality where relief of the pain of
others holds priority. Located in the poor areas of our cities,
they hold special appeal to the young who a looking for a life
of spiritual vision. Among their "graduates" have been some of
the most prophetic voices in American Catholicism such as the
Berrigan brothers, Michael Harrington, and Thomas Merton.
Alternative ritual is a regular part of this community's gospel
sharing. Inspired by the words and example of Dorothy Day,
radical gospel *praxis* lies at the heart of their movement.

In the model of simple living and dedication to the poor
that the Catholic Worker represents there lies the germ for
spiritual renewal of religious orders or their counterparts. I
believe that a very solid argument could be made that most religious orders began like the Catholic Worker—as a kind of
refuge for spirituality and politically disaffiliated persons,

especially the young. Surely Benedict began that way when he left the corruption of Rome to live in a cave as a shepherd in the countryside. This is true of Francis, too, who rejected the affluence of his father for the sake of a band of poor brothers; and Dominic, who rejected the clerical privileges of monks and of canons regular to enter the emerging world of cities and universities. Each of these examples gives evidence of a base community spirit that once inspired religious orders in the Catholic church. When success and institutional cooptation takes over, the base community vision is lost. It seems to me that the key to recovering the true spirit of these early orders can be found in the contemporary struggle for ecological justice, for women's rights, and for human rights in society and church. The latter requires a postclerical base community vision. Dorothy Day, somewhat unwittingly perhaps, incarnated such a vision.

Deep Ecology Communities

As more and more persons awaken to the peril that endangers the earth, a growing number are seeking alternative life-styles that will make for a more responsible way of caring for our natural resources. Community living is such a way, and as ecological consciousness permeates more of our philosophies of education, politics, economics, and religion, groups of persons are banding together. Such communities, bound together by a common struggle for ecological justice, are offering new and futuristic models of base community.

Professions as Base Communities

In the overdeveloped world, the middle class is key to social change, and the key to middle-class life is work and education. Indeed, we could define the middle class's role as (1) educating itself for work; (2) working; and (3) recovering from work. The key to change is to change our work worlds, especially in the professions. More professionals today are sensing the inadequacy of the models on which they are mirroring their work lives. These persons, by linking up with like-minded coworkers, can begin to make a base community within their work environment—one that brings ritual and the new cosmic story, mysticism and heart-work, back to their profession. I believe that of all the base communities I have named, this holds the most promise for the greatest change, since work is where we return our gift to the community. To change work worlds is to change the world.

The Americas in Solidarity

These examples of shared interests between the church of the Americas underline my thesis that it is time for the peoples of the Americas to look more closely at one another's history, to see one another's struggles in light of their own, and to begin to work together.

This is especially possible at the level of ecclesiogenesis, birthing a new way of being church—and of a common spiritual renaissance, a spirituality of creation. In taking on this common vocation and in responding to the signs of our times and to the call of the earth and its Creator, a church of the Americas could return many gifts to the church of Europe and could be a bridge between West and East and between the northern churches and southern churches of Africa, Australia, and New Zealand. Some of the gifts a church of the Americas could return include the spiritual and mystical link with nature; the Cosmic Christ theology that creates a linkage with science, art, and mysticism; the liberation motif not only of the church in Latin America but historically of the slaves in the colonies and of the colonies in North America who struggled against English domination. It could also demonstrate the opportunities available for sharing the wisdom of native peoples, of Celtic peoples, and of women (the feminist movement in the United States is the most theologically advanced in the world); the experience of democracy even in church structures (Anglican and Protestant practices in particular); the emphasis on practice and experience; the urge for a "New Creation," and the prophetic spirit of church history and reform; and an eschatological vision of a wounded earth (Gaia) that yearns for healing.

These gifts are not unique and peculiar to the Americas. Rather they represent much that was lost over the centuries in European Christianity. They are part of the eschatological hope and practice of the church all over the world. This is why the ecclesiogenesis that I envision is not about a schism, but about a renewal of vision, practice, and structure. Liberation theology and creation spirituality are contemporary movements set in different cultural, geographic, and historic contexts, both called to be instruments of global change and healing.

There can be no renaissance in church or society without *moral courage*. And here, especially, the South American people have much to teach us northerners. I recall attending a Liturgy while visiting Bishop Pedro Casadaliga and the eighty church workers who minister with him among the Amazon Indians in Brazil. The theme of that Liturgy was "our martyrs" and each person got up and lit a candle while reciting two names of co-workers of theirs who had been tortured and murdered. It was a very moving evening, and afterward one man told me that the hard part was limiting it to two names. "I know at least ten," he said. Truly the South American church has been in our times a "church of the martyrs" with thousands of peasant and union leaders murdered in Central America, for example. The movie *Romero* recalls the same facts about Archbishop Oscar Romero and the ministers and priests who have been martyred in El Salvador. Six more Jesuits and their housekeeper and daughter are now added to this list of martyrs. If one visits the catacombs in Rome one realizes how great a role the age of the martyrs has played in the consciousness of European Christianity. Yet that time is ended. Who in Rome is being martyred for their faith today? In places like Latin America the gift of the spirit that is courage is being renewed and the blood of the martyrs is calling all persons everywhere to stand up and be counted.

"First World" persons have been among the martyrs in the south—for example, the churchwomen in El Salvador. Martin Luther King, Jr., and others have been martyred in the north. Although there is less likelihood that moral boldness will result in physical death in the "First World," nevertheless there are other "deaths" that overdeveloped peoples risk in choosing to stand for justice: the loss of reputation or job; misunderstanding; rumors; envy; projection; imprisonment; ecclesiastical attack. The blood of the martyrs calls us equally to moral courage in this time and in our context. It is evident that *liberation* is needed in both north and south, in overdeveloped and underdeveloped nations, and in the church that must be birthed from the deep experience of both. Are not each of the issues that we have raised subjects for liberation? Southerners are learning the new cosmology from the north; we northerners need to learn courage from our southern brothers and sisters.

Americans need to reflect on the fact that the concept of liberation theology was not first employed in Latin America in this century. Rather, it was the slaves in North America centuries ago who, hearing the stories of the liberation event of Moses leading his people from Egyptian bondage, launched the first "liberation theology" in the Americas. This theology was passed on mostly in song, and we hear it still in many black spirituals. Perhaps it is time to look anew at some of our most cherished Gospel stories.

A Parable Retold

In the Gospel of Luke we read about a rich man and a poor man whose name was Lazarus. I propose the following updated version of that parable:

> There was a rich nation whose people used to dress
> in whatever clothes they wanted every day and buy
> whatever cars they wanted, which emitted untold
> amounts of carbon dioxide. These people ate beef at

fast-food restaurants whenever they wanted; they
created a whole new industry around beef eating
even when it was grown by tearing down rain forests
where the poor lived in another country far away,
even though it was explained to them how they and
especially their children depended on these very rain
forests so far away for their health.

Now at the rich country's border there lay many
poor countries to the south; these countries were
called "Third World." They were covered with sores
of poverty, unemployment, lack of food and medical
care, and debts owed the rich nation. Much of their
land and soil and forests had been stripped bare by
the nations' companies, who paid to support the dictators and their military guards. The sores of the
"Third World" included five hundred million persons
starving; one billion persons living in absolute poverty; one billion, five-hundred million persons with
no access to basic health care; half a billion persons
with no work and a per capita income of less than
$150 per year; 814 million illiterate persons; two bil-
lion people with no dependable water supply; the
wiping out of forests and the erosion of soil. These
sores and more were present daily for the rich
nations to behold, but they turned their backs and
pretended that such suffering was not "newsworthy."
They built a culture of denial and left the dogs to
lick the sores of the poor.

For years the "Third World" longed to fill itself
with the scraps that fell from the rich nation's table.
But most of the assistance that "Third World"
received from "First World" was in the form of military weapons and money to support dictators and
their armies because their armies were needed to
keep the unhappy people from rebelling. The rich
nation even trained the poor armies in the methods
of effective torture. The rich nation received fruit

and coffee and sugar and cocoa and eventually
cocaine and other drugs to feed all its insatiable
needs.

And the poor nations died and were carried by
the angels to the bosom of Abraham. The rich
nation died and was buried.

In its torment in Hades the rich nation looked
up and saw Abraham a long way off, with the "Third
World" beginning to rise from the dead straight out
of Abraham's bosom. So it cried out, "Father Abraham, pity us and send the 'Third World' to dip the
tip of its finger in water and cool our tongue, for we
are in agony in these flames."

"My child," Abraham replied, "remember that
during your life good things came your way, just as
bad things came the way of 'Third World.' Now the
'Third World' is being resurrected here while you are
in agony. But that is not all: between us and you a
great gulf has been fixed to stop anyone, if they
wanted to, crossing from our side to yours, and to
stop any crossing from your side to ours."

The rich nation replied, "Father, I beg you then
to send 'Third World' to the other nations of the
'First World' since I have five brother nations in our
common alignment—Japan, the European Common
Market, Canada, Australia, New Zealand—to give
them warning so that they do not come to this place
of torment too."

"They have Moses and the prophets of East and
West," said Abraham, "let them listen to them."

"Ah, no, Father Abraham," said the rich nation, "but
if someone comes to them from the dead, they will
repent."

Then Abraham said to the rich nation, "If they will
not listen either to Moses or to the prophets or to Jesus,
they will not be convinced even if someone should rise
from the dead."

In this book I have argued, in effect, that the dominant religious soil in which the West has planted Christianity is in great part exhausted. Those who still wish to follow the message of compassion and the person of Jesus and other prophets of the West are called to do some replanting in richer soil. The church of the Americas offers an opportunity in our time when historical circumstances come together in this hemisphere. Today, "First World" and "Third World" meet so directly; they share a common, dismal future if earth destruction and human destruction cannot be stopped. The largest Christian denomination, that of Roman Catholicism, is conspicuously represented in this hemisphere. If the church of the Americas were to seize this moment in history, for example, with the liberating movement of liberation theology in the Brazilian church and the movement of creation spirituality in the United States, we might all see a renewed expression of religious wisdom.

What I am calling for, a "church of the Americas," has nothing to do with schism or *jingoism*. It has to do with the salvation, the healing of the planet and our peoples before it is too late. It has to do with Good News because no one people—be they the people of Rome or Brazil or the United States—hold any monopoly on the Spirit. It has to do with bridge building between the rapidly passing European era of Christianity to an era that is more representative of the spirituality of the peoples of Asia, Africa, and the Americas. It has to do with realizing that Europeans can take care of Europe but that those in the American hemisphere need to start taking care of the Americas. Why not, for example, let Western Europe create a "Marshall Plan" for Eastern Europeans, but let the United States and Canada create one for Latin America?

The Spirit always blows where it will. Given the historical and geographic confluences of our day, the Spirit may well be asking a great work of spiritual transformation on the part of the people of the Americas.

❖ 9 ❖

Cosmology as Liberation: A Lesson from Job

Job is a person who underwent a profound "dark night of the soul." For no apparent reason—for he was a good and righteous man—his happy life with his family and community was totally destroyed. Chaos displaced order; sadness displaced joy; despair overcame hope; anger overcame his peace; sickness overcame his health. His friends became part of the problem, for they blamed his troubles on his sins or on his bad theology or both. Though he listened to their theories he could not agree with them, and so he took his case to the person in charge, to God. He felt it was all God's doing—and he wanted some answers that made sense (30:19).

It seems to me that in many ways Job represents the northern countries, the more comfortable or so-called "First World" countries of our time. In these cultures there is a kind of chaos replacing order; a sadness displacing joy; a despair overcoming hope; an anger banishing what seemed like a blissful era just thirty years ago; and a sickness overcoming health. These cultures do not feel that they are responsible for their troubles; their efforts to practice democracy and avoid atomic war have largely paid off over the past forty-five years. Yet the "dark night of the soul" has descended on them as they face up to environmental peril, to despair among the young and to demands from the southern or two-thirds of the world that suffers so drastically. Is there a lesson about liberation (otherwise known as redemption) in the Job story?

When Job takes his case to God, God meets him face to face and interrogates him like a prosecuting attorney.

Where were you, Job, when I laid the foundation
of the earth?
Tell me if you have understanding.
Who determined its measurements—surely you know . . .
Or who shut in the sea with doors, when it burst forth
from the womb?
Have you commanded the morning or caused the dawn
to know its place?
Have you comprehended the expanse of the earth?
Declare if you know all this.
Can you hunt the prey for the lion?
Do you know how the mountain goats bring forth?
Do you give the horse its might? (Job 38:4, 8, 12)

God's answer to Job's "dark night of the soul" is to challenge him with the wonder and amazement of the universe. Job is chagrined by this approach—he is learning his place in the universe. He responds:

I am speechless: what can I answer?
I put my hand on my mouth.
I have said too much already;
now I will speak no more. (40:4ff)

In a second encounter, God challenges Job about whether he is powerful enough to wrestle with the powers and principalities and monsters of the universe: "Can you draw out Leviathan with a fishhook or press down his tongue with a cord? Will you play with him as with a bird or will you put a leash on him for your maidens?" (41:1, 5). And again, Job is chagrined, "I have uttered what I did not understand," he confesses.

Here we learn that cosmology—beholding the awe and terror of the universe—leads to clear thinking, to seeing things in perspective, and therefore to repentance. Job is not merely a suffering individual—his plight represents the plight of his people. Why did the Israelites have to suffer so much, why does their innocence have to be exploited by God? Healing is restored when Job and his community see their plight in light of the entire creation. Then happiness returns to Job's life. His healing is not so much a matter of sin or blame as it is of *perspective*. He could not find healing in an anthropocentric view of the world or of the human-divine relationship. The healing comes with the breakthrough of a cosmic awareness. Might a similar story happen for us earth people, almost overcome by the "dark night of our souls," as we learn to let go, to repent, to see anew in light of the awesome gifts of the universe?

Like Job, our species might have a happy ending to its story once we realize what he did: *That his world was too small.* Whenever we attempt to live or practice education, religion, politics, work, or economics without a cosmology, *our world is too small.* If our world is too small, so too are our *souls.* For, as Eckhart says, "Our soul is the world." Our souls are too small—there lies the price we have paid for the human-centeredness of our civilization. How do we enlarge our souls? Cosmology is the corrective to this myopic worldview and the experience of awe is divinity's way of getting through to us yet another time. For awe is not only the response of blessing for blessing; it is also the moment of breakthrough in which all things are rediscovered in their radiance and beauty.

I wonder if the time has not come, in our efforts to move humanity to a fuller expression of its destiny, to begin asking the most basic of all moral questions: How can we honor one another? For "honor" is another word for "reverence," and reverence comes from awe. If we have begun to intuit the awesomeness of the universe and the awesomeness of our being here, then it is time to honor one another.

How can we do this? One way is ask one another to teach us things. During creation spirituality workshops in New Zealand and Australia recently the aboriginal people of each of those lands were invited to speak to the group at large and to lead a seminar. I was struck by what both the Maori leaders and the Aboriginal leaders told me: *That they were moved and honored just to be invited to teach.* And the white folks who became students to these persons grew in the process.

It is time that European Americans honored Native Americans by inviting them to teach us; and Christians honor Jewish people; and men honor women (which is not putting them on pedestals but listening to their experience); and men honor men (is this not at the heart of male liberation movements?); and adults honor the young; and all honor our elders; and the northern, wealthy one-third of the human race honor the southern, poor two-thirds; and humans honor the nonhuman brothers and sisters with whom we share this planet. In this way we will begin to live out the morality that follows from a cosmic spirituality and we will learn to ground our struggle for justice, rights, and responsibilities in the most common ground of all: our shared experience of awe.

Selected Readings

Anderson, William. *Green Man*. San Francisco: HarperCollins, 1990.

Berry, Thomas. *The Dream of the Earth*. San Francisco: Sierra Club Books, 1988.

Berry, Thomas, and Brian Swimme. *The Universe Story*. Forthcoming.

Boff, Leonardo. *Church: Charism & Power*. New York: Crossroad, 1985.

———. *Ecclesiogenesis: The Base Communities Reinvent the Church*. Maryknoll, NY: Orbis, 1986.

———. *When Theology Listens to the Poor*. San Francisco: Harper & Row, 1989.

Boff, Leonardo, and Clodovis Boff. *Introducing Liberation Theology*. Maryknoll, NY: Orbis, 1987.

Bolen, Jean Shinoda. *Gods in Everyman*. San Francisco: Harper & Row, 1989.

Cady, Susan, Marian Ronan, and Hal Taussig. *Sophia: The Future of Feminist Spirituality*. San Francisco: Harper & Row, 1986.

Campbell, Joseph. *The Power of Myth*. New York: Doubleday, 1988.

Cardenal, Ernesto. *Cantico Cosmico*. Managua, Nicaragua: Editorial Nueva Nicaragua, 1989.

Carson, Rachel. *A Sense of Wonder*. New York: Harper & Row, 1956.

Chenu, M. D. *Nature, Man, and Society in the Twelfth Century*. Chicago: University of Chicago Press, 1968.

Cowan, James. *Mysteries of the Dreaming: The Spiritual Life of Australian Aborigines*. Dorset, Great Britain: Prism Press, 1989.

Dillard, Annie. *Pilgrim at Tinker Creek*. New York: Harper & Row, 1974.

———. *The Writing Life*. New York: Harper & Row, 1989.

Douglas-Klotz, Neil. *Prayers of the Cosmos*. San Francisco: Harper & Row, 1990.

Doyle, Brendan. *Meditations with Julian of Norwich*. Santa Fe, NM: Bear & Co., 1983.

Ehrenreich, Barbara. *Fear of Falling: The Inner Life of the Middle Class*. New York: Pantheon, 1989.

Everson, William. *Earth Poetry*. Berkeley: Oyez, 1980.

Fox, Matthew. *Breakthrough: Meister Eckhart's Creation Spirituality in New Translation*. Garden City, NY: Doubleday, 1980.

———. *The Coming of the Cosmic Christ*. San Francisco: Harper & Row, 1988.

————. *Illuminations of Hildegard of Bingen*. Santa Fe, NM: Bear & Co., 1985.

————. *Meditations with Meister Eckhart*. Santa Fe, NM: Bear & Co., 1982.

————. *Original Blessing: A Primer in Creation Spirituality*. Santa Fe, NM: Bear & Co., 1983.

————. *A Spirituality Named Compassion*. San Francisco: Harper & Row, 1990.

————. *Whee, We, wee all the Way Home: A Guide to a Sensual, Prophetic Spirituality*. Santa Fe, NM: Bear & Co., 1981.

Freire, Paulo. "Studies in Adult Education." University of Dar Es Salaam, Institute of Adult Education, 1971.

Gadon, Elinor W. *The Once and Future Goddess*. San Francisco: Harper & Row, 1989.

Heschel, Abraham Joshua. *The Earth Is the Lord's*. New York: Farrar, Straus & Giroux, 1978.

————. *The Prophets*. New York: Harper & Row, 1962.

Jacobi, Jolande, and R. F. C. Hull, eds. *C. G. Jung: Psychological Reflections*. Princeton: Princeton University Press, 1978.

Jantsch, Erich. *The Self-Organizing Universe*. New York: Pergamon Press, 1980.

Kuhn, Thomas. *The Structure of Scientific Revolutions*. Chicago: University of Chicago Press, 1970.

Lernoux, Penny. *People of God: The Struggle for World Catholicism*. New York: Viking, 1989.

Levertov, Denise. *The Poet in the World*. New York: New Directions, 1973.

Lopez, Barry. *Crossing Open Ground*. New York: Vintage Books, 1989.

Macy, Joanna. *Despair and Personal Power in Nuclear Age*. Philadelphia: New Society, 1983.

Maher, John M., and Dennie Briggs, eds. *An Open Life: Joseph Campbell in Conversation with Michael Toms*. New York: Harper & Row, 1990.

Martin, Joseph F. *Foolish Wisdom*. San Jose, CA: Resource Publications, 1990.

Meeker, Joseph W. *The Comedy of Survival*. Los Angeles: Guild of Tutors, 1980.

Merkle, John C. *Abraham Joshua Heschel: Exploring His Life and Thought*. New York: Macmillan, 1985.

————. *The Genesis of Faith: The Depth Theology of Abraham Joshua Heschel*. New York: Macmillan, 1985.

Merton, Thomas. *A Vow of Conversation: Journals 1964–1965*. New York: Farrar, Straus & Giroux, 1988.

Miller, George. "Plight of America's Young Black Men." *Oakland Tribune*, 29 August 1989, A–8.

Mitchell, Stephen, trans. *The Book of Job*. Berkeley, CA: North Point, 1987.

O'Connor, Kathleen M. *The Wisdom Literature*. Wilmington, DE: Michael Glazier, 1988.

Rank, Otto. *Art and Artist*. New York: Agathon Press, 1975.

Richards, M. C. *Centering in Pottery, Poetry, and the Person*. Middletown, CT: Wesleyan University Press, 1964.

Robbins, John. *Diet for a New America*. Walpole, NH: Stillpoint, 1987.

Ruether, Rosemary. *Womanchurch*. San Francisco: Harper & Row, 1985.

Schaef, Anne Wilson. *When Society Becomes an Addict*. San Francisco: Harper & Row, 1987.

Schaef, Anne Wilson, and Diane Fassel. *The Addictive Organization*. San Francisco: Harper & Row, 1988.

Sheldrake, Rupert. *The Presence of the Past*. New York: Times Books, 1988.

———. *The Rebirth of Nature*. New York: Bantam, Forthcoming.

Simpson, Dick. *The Politics of Compassion and Transformation*. Athens, OH: Swallow Press & Ohio University Press, 1989.

Strickland, William. "The Future of Black Men," *Essence*, November 1989, 52ff.

Swimme, Brian. *The Universe Is a Green Dragon*. Santa Fe, NM: Bear & Co., 1985.

Thomas, Lewis. *The Lives of a Cell*. New York: Bantam Books, 1975.

Thomas Aquinas, *Summa Theologiae*. Rome: Marietti, 1952.

Thurman, Howard. *With Head and Heart*. New York: Harcourt, Brace, Jovanovich, 1979.

Woodruff, Sue. *Meditations with Mechtild of Magdeburg*. Santa Fe, NM: Bear & Co., 1982.

About the cover illustration, cover artist Robert Lentz writes:

The ancient Celts envisioned God in feminine symbols as
a trinity. The roles they assigned each person of the trinity
were very similar to those Matthew Fox describes in his
book. The first person, the Virgin, gave birth to the world.
The second person, the Mother, guarded and protected the
world. The third person, the Crone, was a wisdom figure
who also represented the end of all things, death. The snake
and raven were both associated with the female trinity as
symbols of the oneness of life and death: the snake who
grew as she consumed her own tail and the raven who
consumed carrion but flew high into the heavens. I have
depicted the three persons of the trinity from different
races, to reflect a vison of the Godhead beyond any one
culture. I have returned to more ancient feminine sym-
bolism because I believe imagining God in exclusively
masculine symbols has contributed to the plight of the
human race, as described in Fox's book.